STICKMEN'S GUIDE TO
SCIENCE and
TECHNOLOGY
plus ENGINEERING and MATH

by John Farndon
Illustrated by Joe Matthews

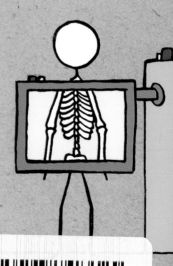

Contents

First published in 2020
by Hungry Tomato Ltd
F1, Old Bakery Studios
Blewetts Wharf, Malpas Road,
Truro, Cornwall, TR1 1QH, UK

Copyright © 2020
Hungry Tomato Ltd

A CIP catalogue record for this book is available from the British Library.
ISBN 978-1-913077-716

Printed and bound in China

Discover more at
www.mybeetlebooks.com

BEETLE
BOOKS

A Journey of Discovery

Follow the Stickmen as they discover science, technology, engineering, and math—all in one great guide. Learn about everything from how to cure life-changing diseases to how to build microscopic robots. Use numbers to create supercomputers or learn how a black hole can suck in a planet. The Stickmen navigate their way through this fascinating world on a journey of discovery.

The Sun is 91 million miles (146 million km) away from us— perfect for keeping us alive and well.

About Science

Scientists are people who explore the world and how it works. They study everything from how microbes grow to what happens when a volcano erupts. They look for patterns and rules that help us understand why things happen and help predict what might happen in the future.

What do scientists do?

Scientists ask questions and then try to answer them with experiments, observations, and mathematical reasoning. Sometimes they work things out on paper, or they try things out in a laboratory. Some scientists go out into the world and collect data.

John Dalton (1766–1844) proposed the theory that chemicals are made from different atoms.

Scientific theories

Scientists like "theories." A theory is a completely worked out explanation of how something works. But a theory is only any good if it can be tested in the real world and is proven right. Newton's theory of gravity shows how things fall. Dalton's atomic theory shows how each chemical **element** has its own unique **atom**.

The scientific method

Scientists like to follow what they call the "scientific method." First, they decide a question to ask, such as "Why does rain fall?" Then, they do some basic thinking and research to come up with a first idea of why, called a hypothesis. Finally, they do tests to see if the hypothesis is right. If the tests work, they tell other scientists so they can try it, too.

Science on the rise

There are nearly 8 million scientists at work around the world today. That's more than 90 percent of the scientists who ever lived. The number of scientific research reports written doubles every nine years. So it's not surprising that scientific breakthroughs are being made faster than ever.

Aristotle, one of the forefathers of natural philosophy

Natural philosophers

There are many different kinds of scientist today, each one specializing in a different field. For example, particle physicists study the parts of atoms and microbiologist study life under a microscope. In the past, however, scientists studied a wide range of subjects and were called "natural philosophers." The term "scientist" was invented in the 1830s.

Things Moving

If nothing moved, the universe would be boring. In fact, it would be dead. It is movement that makes things interesting. That's why physics is the most basic of all sciences. Physics is about movement or, as scientists say, "motion," and it looks at everything from how a baseball spins to how the universe moves.

When the bat hits the ball, the force of the bat swing is transferred to the ball.

Feel the force!

Physicists are especially interested in **forces**. Things move because of forces. A force is basically a push or pull. It makes things accelerate—that is, change speed or direction.

When a baseball player swings the bat, he transfers the force of his muscles to the bat.

Stop and go

Nothing ever moves without force. Things have what is called **inertia** and move only when force gives them a jump-start. But once moving, inertia keeps them moving at the same speed and direction, only changing when force intervenes. This impulse is called **momentum**.

1 When you are high on a swing, you're pulled by gravity, the force that pulls things down.

2 As you swing down, you gain momentum and swing up the other side.

3 As you swing up the other side, gravity reduces your momentum.

4 As gravity pulls you down again, you gain momentum to swing up the other way.

Faster, faster!

"Positive" **acceleration** is when something gets faster. There is also "negative" acceleration—when something gets slower. In fact, physicists call any change in direction acceleration. And any kind of acceleration needs a force.

Acceleration is typically measured in meters per second (a meter equals almost 40 inches).

1 When an archer stretches back a bow, she gives the bowstring stored energy.

Energize!

Besides forces, physicists are obsessed with **energy**. Energy is what you need to exert a force or make things happen, usually by heating it or making it move. Physicists call this doing "work." Movement (kinetic) energy is energy in action—the energy that things have when they're moving. Stored (potential) energy is energy that is stored and ready to use.

2 When the archer lets go, the string's energy gives the arrow movement energy as it flies forward.

Changing energy

The amount of energy that exists is always the same. But it can move (transfer) or change from one form to another (transform). It also continually switches between movement energy and stored energy. Your body gets the energy to move by converting the energy stored in food. But once the task is done, the energy isn't lost—it's simply changed to heat.

Stuff Happens

Matter is every substance in the universe—everything that's not just empty space. It can be anything from solid chunks of metal to wispy clouds of gas, but it is all made up from a range of substances called chemicals. The scientists who study chemicals are called chemists.

In a state

Every substance is made of tiny, tiny parts called **molecules**, which are much, much too small to see! The way these molecules interact means matter comes in three main forms: solid, liquid, and gas. These are called the states of matter. They seem different, but they can switch from one to the other and back if the temperature and pressure is right.

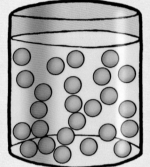

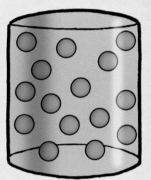

A **solid** has strength and a definite shape, because its molecules are locked together in a regular structure and vibrate on the spot. The hotter it gets, the more they vibrate.

A **liquid** flows into the shape of any container. This is because the bonds between the molecules are loose enough to slide over each other like grains of dry sand.

A **gas** has no shape or strength and swells to fit any space. This is because the molecules move so fast that they do not hold together.

Melting and boiling

When substances warm up, the molecules move more and more. So they go from solid to liquid (melting) and from liquid to gas (evaporation). Once the temperature reaches a certain temperature (boiling point), the liquid will get no hotter and simply evaporates.

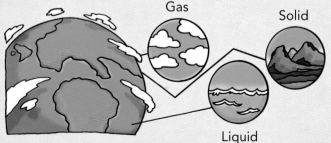

Gas

Solid

Liquid

Condensing and freezing

When substances cool down, the molecules move less. So they change from gas to liquid (known as condensing) and from liquid to solid (freezing).

Seriously tiny!

Matter and molecules are built up from even tinier atoms. Atoms are so tiny that they can be seen only under powerful microscopes—and they're not solid balls, just clumps of energy. Nearly every atom has a "nucleus," or center, made of two kinds of particle: protons and neutrons. Even tinier particles, called electrons, whiz around the nucleus.

Scientists can see atoms (left) with special microscopes (above).

Mixing it up

All the substances in the universe are made from just 120 or so basic chemicals or elements, such as gold and carbon. Each has its own special character and unique kind of atom. Atoms of different elements can join to form combination chemicals called **compounds**. When substances mingle without joining chemically, it's called a mixture.

Pure chemicals
Element: helium
Compound: water

Mixtures
Varied mixture: wet sand
Uniform mixture: tea with sugar

Impure drinks

Even clean water usually contains tiny, invisible traces of other substances. That's why scientists call it a **solution**. A solution is a liquid with solids dissolved in it. When a solid dissolves, it breaks up and vanishes in the liquid but is still there.

- In a solution, solids are dissolved invisibly
- In a colloid, such as milk, tiny solids are mixed in but not dissolved, making the liquid cloudy
- In a suspension, bigger grains of solids float but will eventually sink

Seeing Stars

The few thousand stars you see in the sky at night are just a tiny fraction of the mega-trillions in the universe—and astronomers want to study them all. Astronomy is the oldest of all sciences, but it is now making some of the most exciting of all scientific discoveries.

Day and night

To us on Earth, it looks as if the sun is moving through the sky. But it's really our planet Earth moving while the sun stays still. Earth spins completely around every 24 hours. It turns us to face the sun and then turns us away again, giving us day and night. Earth also goes on a journey around the sun, called its orbit, which takes a year.

Sun time

The direction of the sun changes steadily during the day, moving from east to west across the sky. It moves so steadily, you can tell the time from the direction of your shadow.

Stars wheeling round the North Star, as seen from the Rocky Mountains

Round and round

Earth whirls around the sun along with a small family of planets called the **solar system**. Four small rocky planets, including Earth, orbit close to the sun and four giant gas planets orbit farther out. Most planets are also circled by their own moons, and in between the planets are a lot of lumps called asteroids, as well as icy chunks called comets, which whiz in and out.

Mercury
Venus
Asteroid belt
Jupiter
Uranus

Neptune
Saturn

Mars
Earth

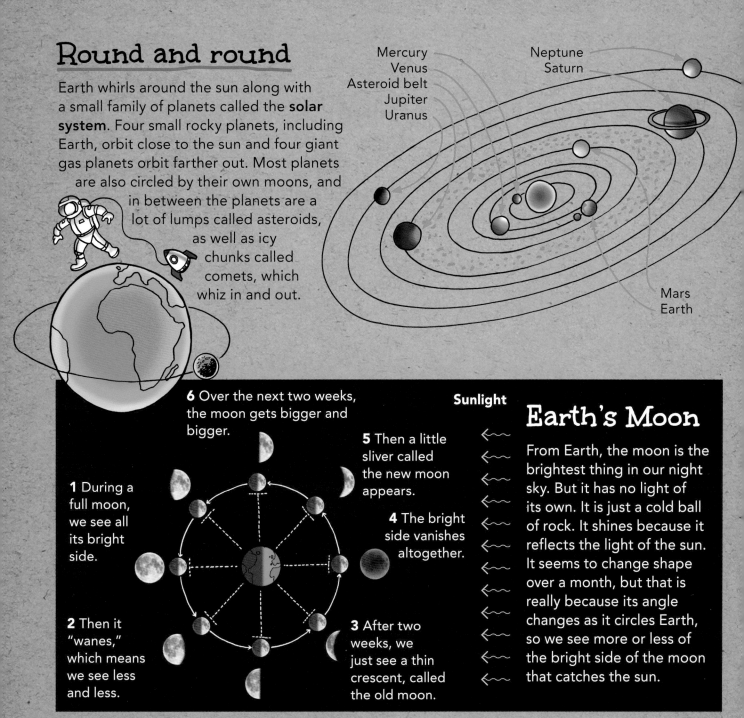

6 Over the next two weeks, the moon gets bigger and bigger.

5 Then a little sliver called the new moon appears.

4 The bright side vanishes altogether.

1 During a full moon, we see all its bright side.

2 Then it "wanes," which means we see less and less.

3 After two weeks, we just see a thin crescent, called the old moon.

Sunlight

Earth's Moon

From Earth, the moon is the brightest thing in our night sky. But it has no light of its own. It is just a cold ball of rock. It shines because it reflects the light of the sun. It seems to change shape over a month, but that is really because its angle changes as it circles Earth, so we see more or less of the bright side of the moon that catches the sun.

Steering by the stars

As Earth turns, the stars seem to wheel slowly through the sky. In fact, they stay in the same place. But in the northern half of the world, there is one bright star, right in the middle of the wheel, which never moves. It is called the North Star, or polestar, and in olden days sailors used it to show them where to find north.

You can find the Pole Star by looking for a distinctive group of stars called the Big Dipper, which points to it.

13

The Deep Blue Sea

Nearly three-quarters of the world is covered by five great oceans: the Pacific, Atlantic, Indian, Southern, and Arctic. They are so deep and dark that we know only a little about them. However, scientists who study oceans (oceanographers) are discovering more and more.

Making waves

Ocean waves begin far out in the ocean, as winds blow the surface into ripples. The ripples pile up into waves called swell. The water in waves barely moves, just rolling around as they swell up and passing on their energy to the next wave. But as they near the coast, waves pile up and spill over to "break" on to the shore in an avalanche of foam.

Coastal zone — Pelagic zone (open ocean)

Continental shelf

Top (euphotic) layer

Middle (bathyal) layer

Deep (abyssal) layer

The depths of the ocean

Around each ocean is a narrow rim where the sea is shallow, called the continental shelf. Beyond it, the seafloor plunges thousands of feet to the vast slime-covered abyssal plain. If you dived down in the ocean, you'd find it getting darker and darker, and the creatures getting stranger and stranger.

Deep pressure

As you go deeper in the ocean, the water squeezes harder. Submarines can go down about 3,280 feet (1 km) before the pressure begins to crush them. You can see how pressure increases with depth by using a plastic bottle or cardboard carton.

1 Make three equal holes in a row on the carton: one at the top, one in the middle, and one at the bottom. Tape over the holes with adhesive tape.

2 Place the carton in a basin. Fill it with water, then quickly pull off the tape to open the holes.

3 See how the water squirts out much farther from the bottom hole, because of the greater pressure.

Full moon

New moon

Tides are at their most extreme twice a month, during "spring tides," when the moon is in line with the sun and they pull together.

First quarter moon

Third quarter Moon

In between, there are more moderate "neap tides," when the moon and sun pull at right angles.

Tide's up

Tides are the rise and fall of the sea that happens twice every day. They are caused by the pull of gravity between the earth and moon. This stretches the ocean out in line with the moon, so there is one high tide on the side of Earth nearest the moon and another on the far side. This tidal bulge moves around Earth as the planet turns, bringing high tides twice daily.

Why is the sea salty?

The sea is salty because rivers carry the salty parts of dissolved rock into the sea. Over time, enough salt has washed into the sea to cover the entire world in salt to a depth of 500 feet (150 m)!

You're My World

We humans have been living on Earth a long, long time. But it's only in recent years that Earth scientists and geologists (rock scientists) have begun to discover how its landscapes are shaped, and how it is all put together.

World on a plate

Earth's surface is cracked into giant slabs of rock called **tectonic plates** that are forever shifting around the world, carrying the continents with them. There are seven gigantic plates, ten smaller plates, and dozens of "micro" plates.

The biggest plate is the Pacific Plate under the Pacific Ocean.

All the other major plates carry continents.

Hot mountains

Volcanoes are places where red-hot liquid rock (magma) from the mantle bursts onto the surface. Sometimes the magma oozes out slowly. Sometimes it explodes, blasting out ash, gases, and lava. The world's 500 or so "active" volcanoes lie mostly along the cracks between tectonic plates, especially in a "Ring of Fire" (in red on the map above) around the Pacific Ocean.

What's inside?

Earth is similar to an egg. It has a thin shell of tough rock called the crust; a **mantle** (the egg white) of hot, half-melted rock; and a superhot metal "core" (the yolk) of iron and nickel. The mantle is continually churning about, moving the plates on the surface and setting off volcanoes and earthquakes. The circulation of the metal core makes Earth magnetic.

Continent

Ocean

Lithosphere (the crust and the stiff upper part of the mantle)

Crust

Mantle

Asthenosphere (the semi-molten upper part of the mantle)

Lower mantle

Liquid outer core

Core

Solid inner core

Shaky ground

The worst earthquakes occur in earthquake zones along boundaries between tectonic plates. They are set off when the plates suddenly jolt past each other. The jolt sends shock waves or "seismic waves" through the ground. Earthquake scientists monitor the ground all the time for slight movements showing a 'quake might be on its way.

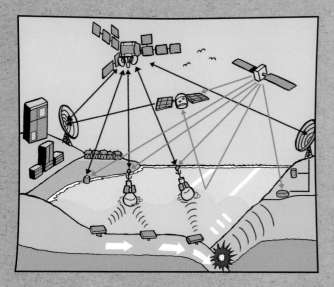

Make your own weather station

You can make your own weather station to record the changes in weather through the year. The basic equipment can be bought inexpensively online. You will need:

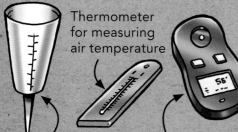

Thermometer for measuring air temperature

Rain gauge for collecting rain

Anemometer for measuring the wind

Something in the air

"Meteorologists" (weather scientists) study the atmosphere to warn if a storm is on its way. They are helped by satellite pictures that show shifting clouds, and by computers that process data from thousands of weather stations on atmospheric conditions, including temperature, moisture content, air pressure, and wind.

That's Life

The variety of life on Earth is amazing, so biologists (scientists who study living things) have a lot to study. More than 1.25 million species of animal, 391,000 plants, and 10,000 microbes are known, and some biologists think there are trillions we've yet to discover.

Cells are the building blocks of life.

Cells build to make tissues, such as skin.

Tissues make organs, such as the brain or heart.

Building life

Amazingly, all living things or "organisms" are made from tiny cells that can be seen only under a microscope. The simplest organisms, such as bacteria, consist of just one cell. More complex creatures are made by a lot of different kinds of cells growing together. We humans are made from 37.2 trillion cells!

Animals and plants make communities.

Organs and tissues combine to make animals and plants.

Life packages

All cells have the same basic structure: a thin skin or membrane wrapped around a gelatin-like mixture of chemicals called the cytoplasm. This contains various structures called organelles. Plant and animal cells have a control center, or nucleus; bacteria and similar organisms do not.

Plant cells have:

Tough outer wall of cellulose

Organelles called chloroplasts, which trap the sun's energy

Large space filled with air or water called a vacuole

Nucleus

Animal cells have:

Soft membrane with no rigid wall

Tiny vacuoles

Nucleus

Variety of organelles

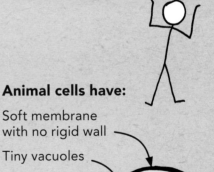

Animal cells

An animal cell is a tiny chemical factory containing a variety of organelles, each with its own function.

Mitochondria are the cell's power stations.

The nucleus controls what chemicals are made.

Lysosomes break down and absorb materials taken in by the cell.

The rough endoplasmic reticulum (ER) is the cell's chemical assembly line.

Vesicles move assembled chemicals for despatch.

The golgi apparatus makes chemicals ready for use or export.

Ribosomes build chemicals.

Animal watching

Botanists study plants and zoologists study animals. Often zoologists learn about animals by watching them, from secret observation points called hides, as they go about their lives. Remote control cameras help get good pictures without disturbing the animals.

Growing a bean

Even the biggest, most complex living thing starts small and simple. You can see for yourself how an entire plant grows from just a tiny bean.

1 Roll a piece of paper towel and slip it inside a glass jar.

2 Slip a bean between the jar and paper, halfway down the jar.

3 Put a few tablespoons of water into the jar and place it in a cupboard or other dark place.

4 After a week, remove the jar from the cupboard. Plant the shoot in a flowerpot of soil and place it on a windowsill.

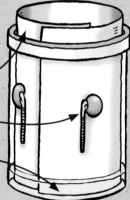

Home Ground

Most plants or animals are choosy. They have their own natural place or "habitat" in the world and can live well only there. Their chosen habitat may be the mattress on your bed, for a bedbug, or the whole of the Arctic, for a polar bear.

Natural regions

The world's weather varies from the bitter chill of the polar regions to the scorching heat of tropical deserts. The typical weather in a place is called its climate. Different climates create natural regions called **biomes**, each home to its own unique range of plants and animals, such as those shown in the diagram. The oceans are the biggest natural biomes of all.

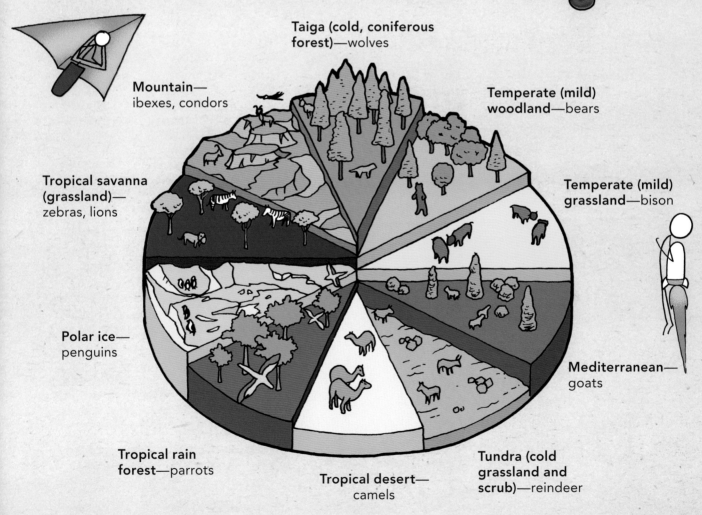

Taiga (cold, coniferous forest)—wolves

Mountain— ibexes, condors

Temperate (mild) woodland—bears

Tropical savanna (grassland)— zebras, lions

Temperate (mild) grassland—bison

Polar ice— penguins

Mediterranean— goats

Tropical rain forest—parrots

Tropical desert— camels

Tundra (cold grassland and scrub)—reindeer

Map legend

- Tundra
- Taiga
- Temperate woodland
- Tropical forest
- Desert
- Tropical grassland (savanna)
- Temperate grassland (prairie, steppe)

Animal homes

Each continent has a range of biomes, except for Antarctica, which is entirely within the polar biome.

Life systems

Plants and animals survive by living together in interacting communities called **ecosystems**. They pass around between them vital substances, such as carbon, oxygen, and water. They provide food for each other, and the way that plants and animals are linked together by eating each other is called a food chain.

Plants, such as trees, are **"producers,"** because they can make their own food from sunlight.

Losing animals

Human activity is now so intense, with expanding cities, increased pollution, and demands for food and produce, that natural habitats, such as rain forests, are being destroyed rapidly. As a result, many animal species are in danger of dying out, including such wonderful animals as polar bears and rhinos. Some experts believe that more than one-third of all species will be lost in the next 40 years.

"Consumers" eat other living things for food.

"Primary" consumers, such as rabbits eat producers (plants).

"Secondary" consumers eat primary consumers, for example, foxes eat rabbits.

"Decomposers" in the soil, such as bacteria and fungi, break down the remains of living things, such as fallen leaves.

Life Matters

Living things are alive for only a short while. But their kind lives on, because they "reproduce," or make copies of themselves. Plants make seeds from which new plants grow. Animals have babies.

The instruction book

Inside every living cell is a remarkable spiral-shaped molecule called **DNA**. DNA contains all the instructions the cell needs to live, as well as all the instructions to make an exact copy of itself. Like a computer, DNA carries instructions in code. The code is given by the order in which simple chemicals called bases are arranged.

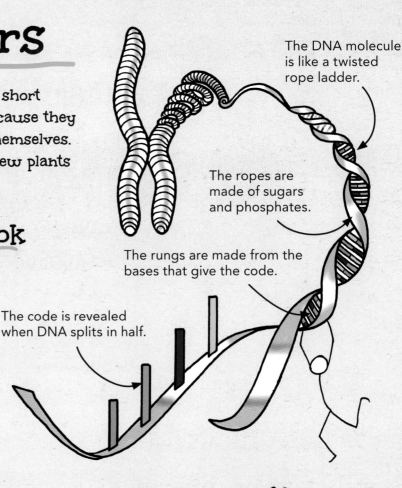

The DNA molecule is like a twisted rope ladder.

The ropes are made of sugars and phosphates.

The rungs are made from the bases that give the code.

The code is revealed when DNA splits in half.

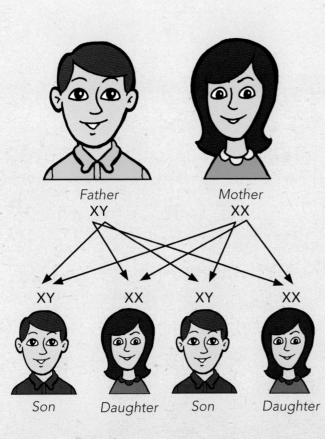

Father
XY

Mother
XX

XY — Son
XX — Daughter
XY — Son
XX — Daughter

Who's a male and who's a female?

Our DNA is packaged in 46 bundles called chromosomes. Typically, girls have 23 matching pairs; boys 22, plus two odd ones: one X shape, the other Y shape. Most girls have two X chromosomes; most boys an X and a Y. A dad's XY and a mom's XX mix and match so they have boys or girls as children. Other mixes (such as XYY) are rare, but possible.

Genes

The DNA code is arranged in genes. Each gene is the instructions for a particular feature in your body. You get one set from your mom and one from your dad. With some features, the two work together. With others, either your mom's or dad's wins out. A gene that always wins, such as the gene for brown eyes, is a "dominant" gene; one that loses is a "recessive" gene. A recessive gene will win if paired with the same gene.

Flower colors

In this diagram, each flower shares its genes for color with another flower to pass on to the next generation. Purple is a dominant gene and white recessive. Only when there is no purple gene will the flower actually turn out white.

Purple (P) = dominant gene

White (w) = recessive gene

PP (purple flower)   Pw (purple flower)

PP (purple flower)   PP (purple flower)   Pw (purple flower)   ww (white flower)

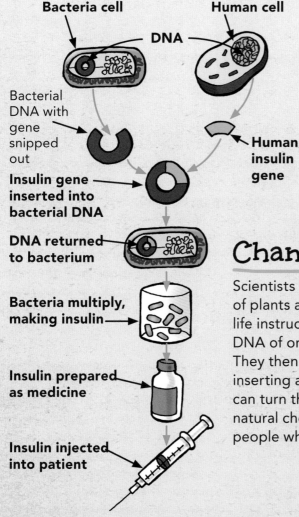

Bacteria cell   **Human cell**

DNA

Bacterial DNA with gene snipped out

Insulin gene inserted into bacterial DNA

Human insulin gene

DNA returned to bacterium

Bacteria multiply, making insulin

Insulin prepared as medicine

Insulin injected into patient

Changing genes

Scientists have learned how to alter the genes of plants and animals to give them different life instructions. They snip the gene from the DNA of one organism using biological scissors. They then insert it into the other organism. By inserting a gene in the DNA of bacteria, they can turn the bacteria into factories for making natural chemicals, such as insulin for treating people who have the disease diabetes.

Your Body

Some are big. Some are small. Some are tall. Some are short. But all our bodies work in the same way. The study of body processes is called physiology, and the study of the way the body is put together is called anatomy.

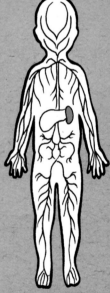

Body systems

The body is made up of a range of interlocking systems, each with a particular task. Some extend through the whole body, such as the skeleton, muscles, and nerves. Others, such as digestion, are localized.

Whole systems

 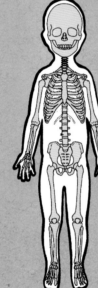

Your muscles enable you to move.

Your skeleton, or framework of bones, supports your body and protects organs.

Your heart and blood circulation supply body cells with oxygen and food.

Your nervous system is the brain and nerves that sense the world and control your body.

Your lymphatic system carries fluid that helps fight disease and clean out waste.

Local systems

 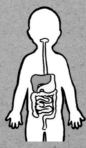 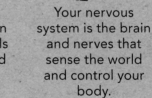 

Respiratory (breathing) system

Hormone (chemical message) system

Digestive system

Excretory (waste) system

Reproductive system

Cell-making machine

Your body is an amazing, around-the-clock, cell-making machine. Every moment of your life, it is making millions of new cells as old ones die. That's how you stay alive and healthy—and it is how you grow. Before you're born, you have special cells that can split to form any kind of cell. Later, most cells are specialized.

Your life begins with stem cells

Stem cells, from which other cells can grow

Blastocysts (new baby cells)

Nerve cells

Heart muscle cells

Red blood cells

Tonsils

Lymphatic vessels

Thymus

Lymph nodes

Spleen

Appendix

Bone marrow

Fighting illness

Every now and then, your body comes under attack from germs, such as bacteria and viruses, that cause disease. Fortunately, it has an array of clever defenses to deal with them, if they ever get in. At the center of this is the lymphatic system and an array of special cells called lymphocytes, made in certain places around the body.

Looking into it

In the past, scientists found out about the body mostly by cutting into corpses. Now, they can see inside living bodies with an array of imaging devices, such as X-rays, MRI scans, PET scans, and CT scans. These penetrate the body with invisible rays to make pictures of what's going on inside.

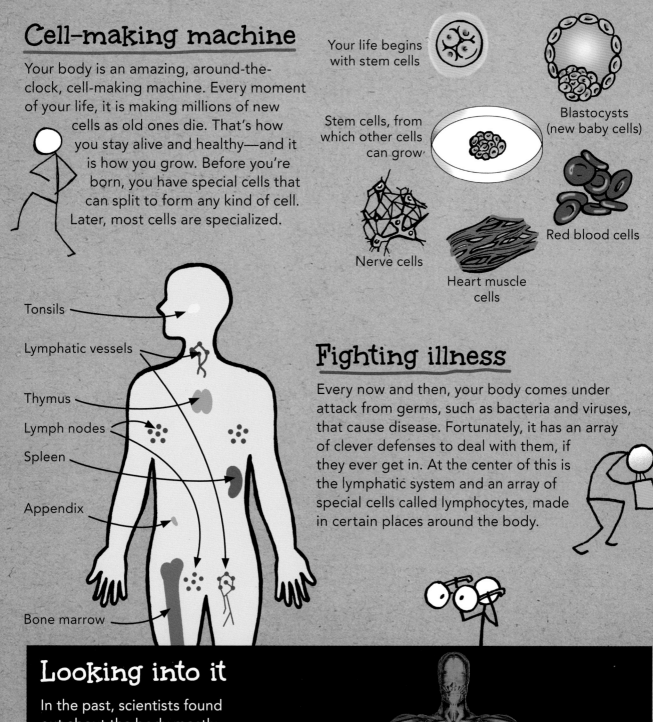

About Technology

Technology is all the smart ways people come up with for making things work. It is about ingenious machines and processes. It is about using scientific knowledge and practical know-how to think up new inventions and methods of dealing with practical problems. It is what makes the modern world tick.

What does technology do?

Technology is about finding practical solutions to problems, as well as finding ways to perform practical tasks better. For instance, you might want to get a lot of people to the top of a mountain quickly, every day. So technologists devised a cable car.

Changing technology

Technology is always changing. Once, gas-engine cars seemed a great technology for enabling people to move quickly anywhere they want. But now we know that the pollution they cause damages the world's climate. So technologists are developing new and cleaner ways of powering cars, such as electric motors and hydrogen fuel cells.

Cutting-edge technology

The newest developments in technology are called cutting-edge technology. That's because they seem like the edge of the blade of a knife, cutting through today's problems to find exciting new solutions. Electric flying taxis are cutting-technology that may soon become a reality.

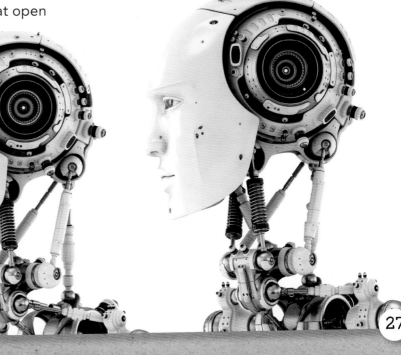

High tech

High tech is the most complicated and clever technology that only specialists can create. Typically, it means technology that needs sophisticated electronic systems, such as robotics, the latest computers, nuclear weapons systems, hospital scanners, and so on. California's Silicon Valley is one of the hubs of high-tech development.

New technology

Every now and then, ideas emerge that open up entirely new areas of technology. It is not always easy to predict which will develop. But here are a few that might: driverless trucks; computers that can teach themselves; **gene** therapy (illnesses cured by altering genes); and face recognition (electronic systems that can identify you from your face alone).

Life Changing

Did you know that with genetic modification (GM), farmers could one day grow chocolate-flavored strawberries? Or that goat milk could be used for bulletproof vests? Genes are the chemical instructions that tell living things how to live and grow. GM is how scientists alter them to make things grow in different ways.

Going for growth

Genes are strips of **DNA**, the chemical molecule inside every living cell that carries life's instructions. Each gene gives a living thing a particular characteristic. To make a change, scientists find a gene that gives the right quality in another organism. They then snip it out chemically and insert it into the DNA of the organism they want to modify.

Human cell

Bacteria cell

1 Scientists take the gene they need from one organism.

2 They insert the gene into the DNA of a cell they want to modify.

3 The cell's DNA now includes the new gene.

4 When the cell multiplies, it has the new characteristic.

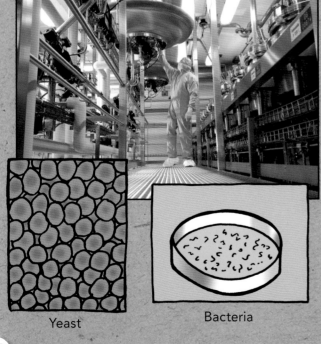

Yeast

Bacteria

Crops

What changes

Bacteria and yeast are typically modified to make them into tiny factories, creating a lot of a particular natural chemical as they multiply, such as human growth hormone or insulin. Farm crops and occasionally animals are modified to give them qualities that will help them grow better.

Animals

New plants

Cotton, potato, and other crops have been given a "Bt" gene to make them poisonous to insects that usually eat them. Some people believe that GM will give us more food to help us feed the world's hungry. But others argue that changing genes could have terrible, unforeseen effects on wildlife.

Copy sheep

An animal born in the normal way has a mix of genes from its mother and father, and so a mix of their characteristics. But animals can be cloned. Cloning means they grow from DNA taken from just one animal, so they are identical copies. The first cloned farm animal was a sheep called Dolly born in 1996.

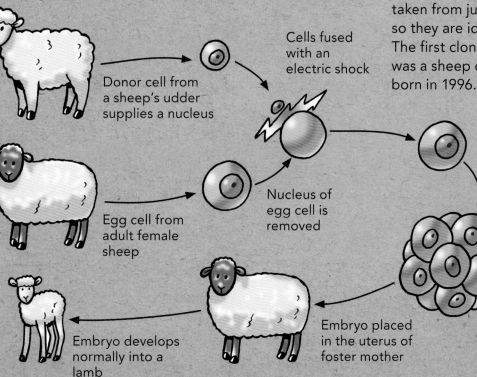

Donor cell from a sheep's udder supplies a nucleus

Egg cell from adult female sheep

Nucleus of egg cell is removed

Cells fused with an electric shock

Fused cells begin dividing normally

Embryo placed in the uterus of foster mother

Embryo develops normally into a lamb

Glowing mice

GM can give animals and plants qualities they never had before. Some mice and other animals have been given a gene that makes jellyfish glow in the dark. So the mice glow in the dark, too. Maybe in future, there will be people who glow in the dark.

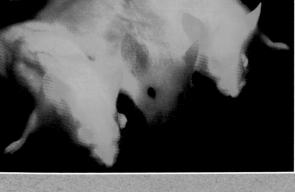

Know All

Computers are already used for an incredibly wide range of tasks, from running train networks to creating movies and music—not to mention the Internet. And they've only just got started.

Your bathroom mirror will give medical advice after scanning your body.

Smart fabrics will adjust the warmth of your clothes to suit the temperature.

Linked-in house

Until recently, the Internet was only a way of communicating between computers and smartphones. But experts expect the **Internet of Things** to expand dramatically. This connects the Internet to ordinary items around the home and office, from refrigerators to TVs, so that your refrigerator, say, could detect when you run out of milk and order it online.

Smart books automatically display 3D and virtual-reality pictures.

Your living room might surround you with sights and sounds from your friend's house or the Amazon jungle.

Tables detect what food is on them, keeping coffee cups hot and iced drinks cold.

Number crunchers

A computer handles data in four stages: input, memory, processing, and output. In the memory and processor, everything is converted to calculations and works by switching patterns of electronic circuits. A computer can only switch electric circuits on or switch them off. So, all its operating instructions are in simple binary (or two-part) code, normally written as 0s and 1s.

Input: A keyboard or camera

Memory

Processor: Control unit and arithmetic logic unit

Output: A screen or printer

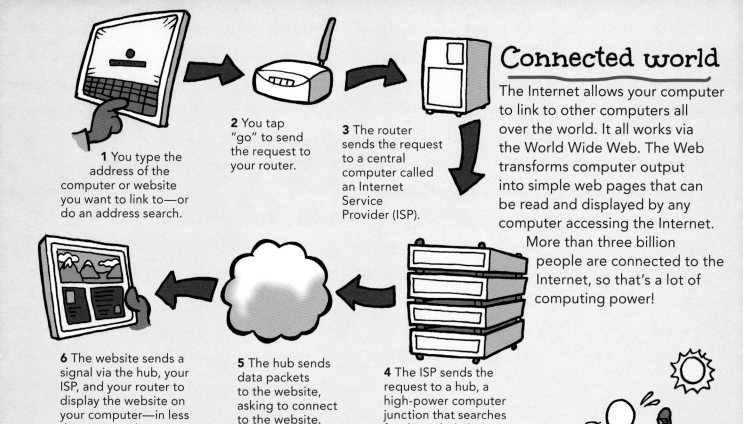

1 You type the address of the computer or website you want to link to—or do an address search.

2 You tap "go" to send the request to your router.

3 The router sends the request to a central computer called an Internet Service Provider (ISP).

Connected world

The Internet allows your computer to link to other computers all over the world. It all works via the World Wide Web. The Web transforms computer output into simple web pages that can be read and displayed by any computer accessing the Internet. More than three billion people are connected to the Internet, so that's a lot of computing power!

6 The website sends a signal via the hub, your ISP, and your router to display the website on your computer—in less than a second.

5 The hub sends data packets to the website, asking to connect to the website.

4 The ISP sends the request to a hub, a high-power computer junction that searches for the right link.

What will the weather be?

Some of the world's most powerful computers are involved in predicting how climate may change in the future. Scientists feed in huge amounts of data about how weather has changed in the past, then get the computer to run these changes into the future. In this way, NASA scientists predict how global temperatures will change.

Superbrain

The world's fastest computer—and the first one as fast as a human brain—is the gigantic Sunway TaihuLight in China. It can perform 93 million billion operations a second. Scientists are using it to rec-reate the first moments of the universe.

Taihu is as fast as a human brain, but soon supercomputers may be as fast as a city full of brains.

Tiny, Tiny

With a powerful microscope, you can see some amazingly small things, from bacteria to the hair cells on a fly. But there's a whole new scale of much smaller things called the nanoscale. Scientists are exploring it to see if they can create the tiniest machines and material structures ever. This is called nanotechnology.

Onsite repairs

Just imagine—in the future, there may be tiny nanomachines that can be sent inside your body to see what's wrong, and even make repairs on the spot. Minute robot submarines could travel around in your blood and send signals back to tell physicians just what's going on. Here's some of the things nanotechnology might do (right).

Nanomachines might work on the inside of your brain to repair brain cells.

A bionic lens could adjust automatically to give you perfect vision.

Nanomaterials could rebuild damaged skin, bone, and tissue.

Nanosensors could detect cancer cells with extreme accuracy, then direct nanomachines to destroy them.

Tiny sensors could respond to changes in the blood and trigger medication.

Water molecule		10^{-1} nm
Gold atom		3×10^{-1} nm
Glucose molecule		1 nm
Hemoglobin		5 nm
Virus		100 nm
Bacteria		1,000 nm
Blood cells		1,000 nm
Hair		100,000 nm
Ant		10^6 nm
Baseball		10^8 nm

Fullerene

Carbon nanotube

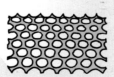
Graphene

How small is nano?

You might think a strand of your hair is pretty thin. Or that bacteria are seriously tiny. But on the nanoscale, hairs are like huge tree trunks and bacteria are like basketballs. A nanometer (nm) is a billionth of a meter (a few inches more than a yard). A hair is actually 100,000 nm across. Scientists are now making nanomaterials of carbon, such as "fullerene" balls, "graphene" sheets, and superstrong "nanotube" fibers.

 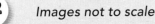 *Images not to scale*

It's a stickup

Geckos can hang onto almost any surface. This is because of tiny forces created between the surface and countless nanoscale projections on hairs on the geckos' feet. Scientists have used this idea to create "gecko tape," which clings to any surface. They hung a toy Spider-Man to glass with it. Now scientists have gecko gloves that let them climb up sheer glass walls.

Seeing tiny

Special, super-powerful "electron" microscopes let you see tiny things, such as the multiple eyes of a fly. But to see and change things on the nanoscale, scientists have developed more powerful magnifiers called atomic force microscopes (AFMs) and scanning tunneling microscopes (STMs), which use special electronic effects. With these, they can push atoms around and arrange them to make tiny machines.

Cutting-edge technology

When knights came up against Muslim warriors in the medieval crusades, they found the Muslims had swords made of "Damascus steel." These swords were so sharp, they could slice through a silk scarf floating through the air (as well as a knight). Recently, scientists found that they owed their sharpness to carbon nanotubes in the steel created by a special forging process.

Self-Control

Mechanical moving figures, called automatons, date back thousands of years. But with computer technology, we can now build smart robots. Robots are machines run by electronic programs that can do complex tasks by themselves. There are already robots making cars and exploring volcanoes. In the future, maybe robots will look and think like us.

Microphones in the ears respond to sounds, such as people speaking.

Cameras in the eyes respond to visual input, recognizing faces and reading books.

Loudspeakers allow for the robot to talk.

The robot walks and balances on two legs.

Hands can grip and sense things by touch.

Bots are us

All robots have three main elements: a controller or "brain"; mechanical parts, such as motors and grippers; and sensors that respond to changes. They can be built in any shape. But many robot makers want to make a "humanoid" robot the same shape as us, with two legs and two arms, such as the famous Japanese Asimo and French Nao robots.

Bots to the rescue

Robots are now being built to perform rescue missions, because they can go where it is too dangerous for people to go. They might find buried earthquake victims or carry medical supplies to people who are trapped. Robots shaped like snakes, called snakebots, can slither under piles of rubble or through pipes on rescue missions.

Robotoys

More robots are being made as toys. For those who cannot have a real dog, Chip the robot dog could be a good alternative. Chip follows you around like a real puppy, with advanced sensors for finding its way around obstacles. It responds to commands. You can even train it to do tricks.

Space bots

At the moment, it is impossible for humans to go to Mars and come back. But robots, such as Curiosity Rover, can be landed there. Curiosity can move around the planet's surface on its six wheels, beaming back pictures and picking up samples for analysis. In 2018, Curiosity found some rock samples with squiggles, which some say are possibly fossils of microscopic life.

Robo-animals

Animals have evolved over millions of years to be especially good at certain things, so robot makers are beginning to look to them for ideas. Here are some of the other robot animals that scientists are developing. They may not look much like the animals, but they move and behave in the same way.

Robot ants can move together in a swarm to pull things as big as cars.

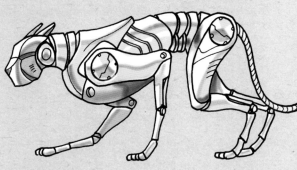

Robot cheetahs are the fastest running robots, reaching nearly 30 miles per hour (50 km/h). They can jump over fences.

Kangaroo robots can jump like real kangaroos, but tirelessly.

Robot butterflies flutter through the air just like real butterflies.

Full-size robot horses can use special sensors to track criminals across snow, ice, and rocky terrain.

Look Over

We live in a world full of electronic pictures. Cameras on our phones allow us to record everyday moments at the touch of a button. But there are many other kinds of electronic picture, from airport security scans to thermal images, which help police to chase suspects in pitch darkness by detecting body heat.

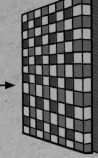

Lens

Three colour filters

Image sensors

Image processor

Output

Electric pictures

Inside your phone there is a rectangle made up of a lot of tiny **photo cells**. When you take a picture, the phone's lens projects a picture onto the cells. The cells respond instantly by sending tiny electric signals that match the pattern of light in the picture. These signals are stored in the phone's memory or display the picture by using the electricity to make a glowing pattern on the screen.

The scanner reveals the contents for the operator.

Travel safe

All major airports have scanners to make sure passengers don't carry anything dangerous onto the plane. Passengers have to step through detectors that pick up even the tiniest piece of metal. Meanwhile, their hand luggage is slid through a tunnel called a computer tomography (CT) scanner. It has a mechanism that turns around your bag while firing X-rays to create a picture of the inside. This reveals any suspicious objects on the watchful officer's screen.

Lead-filled rubber curtains stop the harmful rays from escaping.

Storm warning!

Doppler radar detects things by bouncing microwaves off them. It then builds up a picture from the pattern of waves bouncing back. With a special kind of doppler radar, storm watchers can build up a detailed map of where and how much rain is falling. Doppler radar can even give an indication of wind speed.

Microwaves bounce off drops of water and ice. They are detected by the scanner below.

Doppler radar sends out microwaves.

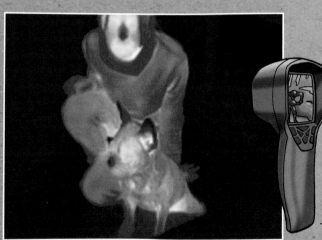

Seeing hot

When things are hot, they send out invisible "infrared" rays. These are like a glowing light, but you cannot see them. However, they can be detected on **thermal imaging** cameras. Cameras such as these can show people in pitch darkness, because of their body heat. Police often use them to catch criminals who think they are hidden by darkness.

Thermal imager

Can't see me!

Scientists are also developing devices to make things invisible. You may think an invisibility cloak is just Harry Potter magic. But scientists are now developing "meta" materials that divert light rays—and really could make you invisible.

Atomic

Atoms are seriously tiny. But the energy that binds together the nucleus or core of an atom is stupendous. By releasing the energy from the nuclei of millions of atoms, nuclear power stations can generate a lot of power.

Power from atoms

Inside a nuclear "reactor" are rods of uranium fuel. When the power station starts to operate, engineers start a **chain reaction** in the rods (below). Special **control rods** soak up some of the stray particles. They get hot and heat water to make steam, which drives turbines that generate electricity.

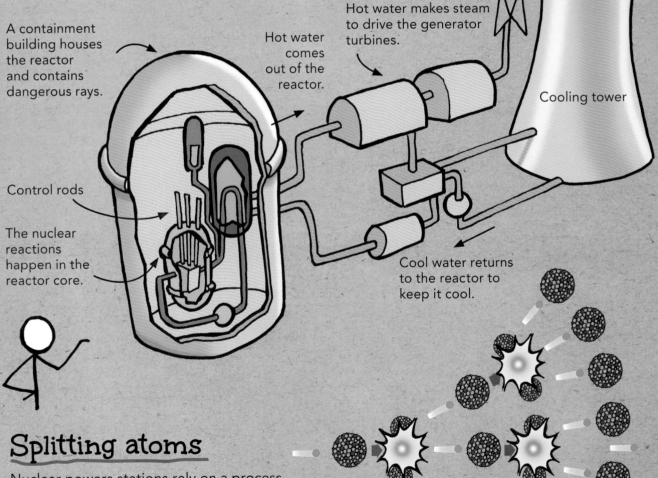

A containment building houses the reactor and contains dangerous rays.

Control rods

The nuclear reactions happen in the reactor core.

Hot water comes out of the reactor.

Hot water makes steam to drive the generator turbines.

Cooling tower

Cool water returns to the reactor to keep it cool.

Splitting atoms

Nuclear powers stations rely on a process called **nuclear fission**. This involves splitting the nuclei of big atoms, such as uranium. To split the nuclei, particles called neutrons are fired at them. As they crash in, they split off other neutrons, which shoot off to split other nuclei. And so it all spreads in a chain reaction.

Nuclear waste

The big problem with nuclear power is that the fuel, once used, becomes highly radioactive: that is, it sends out dangerous rays. When it first comes out of the reactor, it would kill you in seconds if you stood close. It remains radioactive for thousands of years. No one yet knows what to do with the waste. Mostly, it is hidden in special cases underground (right). But these may leak in time.

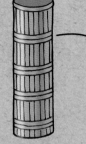

Radioactive fuel bundle

Copper container

Placement room and borehole

Nuclear fusion process

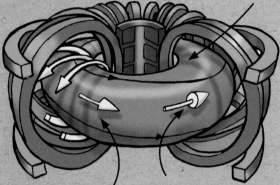

Torus

Magnets speed the gas particles round and round.

Speeding gas particles smash together to release power.

Forced together

Scientists are working to get nuclear power from **nuclear fusion**— hat is, by forcing together small atoms, such as deuterium (a kind of gas). This is the process that makes stars burn bright. Scientists are trying to do it inside a ring-shape tunnel called a torus. If they succeed, they can make a lot of power without dangerous waste.

Before explosion

Detonation

Fission

Fusion

Explosive power

The most devastating bombs ever made combine nuclear fission and nuclear fusion. They are called hydrogen bombs and start with an explosive fission chain reaction. This forces hydrogen atoms together in the core of the bomb to unleash an even more terrible fusion explosion. Fortunately, they have only been exploded for tests.

Look Out

Every now and then, places around the world are hit by extreme natural disasters, such as hurricanes, volcanoes, earthquakes, tsunamis, and floods. There is a much better chance of people escaping if they can be warned in time. So scientists and technologists are working to set up warning systems.

Hurricane watch

Every year, hurricanes sweep across the Atlantic and Pacific oceans. Scientists can follow their paths from satellites high above them. But they cannot measure conditions deep inside the storms. So planes are flown right into them to make observations and drop tubes called "dropsondes," which send data back to storm watchers.

The dropsonde's fall is slowed by a parachute.

GPS gives an accurate position.

Radio transmitters beam out data.

Sensors measure air pressure, temperature and moisture.

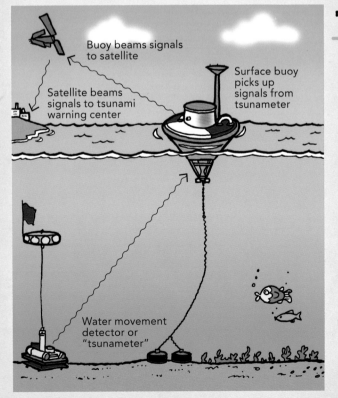

Buoy beams signals to satellite

Satellite beams signals to tsunami warning center

Surface buoy picks up signals from tsunameter

Water movement detector or "tsunameter"

Tsunami warning

Tsunamis are huge waves set off by undersea earthquakes. They move fast, and it is hard to know they are coming. So scientists try to give advance warning by setting up an array of buoys tethered above monitors placed on the seafloor. These detect any dramatic movement of the water and beam out a warning.

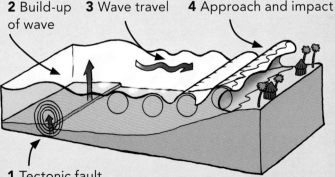

2 Build-up of wave   **3** Wave travel   **4** Approach and impact

1 Tectonic fault

Building safe

The biggest danger in an earthquake is from falling buildings. So in earthquake zones, tall buildings are often built in a way that will withstand quakes. They may not survive the most severe ones, but they can endure most minor quakes.

Cross-bracing gives walls maximum strength.

Steel bars in the walls reduce rocking movements.

Springlike shock absorbers under the building soak up the ground movement, so the building keeps still.

Changes in gases coming out of the volcano may indicate that magma is moving up the vent.

Drones, satellites, and helicopters look for changes from a safe distance.

Shaking of the ground detected by seismometers may show an eruption is imminent.

Meters may detect a slight change in the ground shape, indicating magma pushing up from below.

Volcano warnings

Volcanic eruptions are among the most terrifying of all natural disasters. But many cities are built close to volcanoes. So volcano experts look for warning signs that a volcano might erupt, such as pressure building up in the magma chamber beneath the volcano, or unusual gases being released.

Flood warning

Floods can be slow to start but turn into the most devastating disasters of all, because their effects are so widespread. The flood of the Yangtze River in China in 1931 was the worst ever natural disaster, killing 4 million people. Weather watchers join with river experts to try to warn people of a flood, but even with warning, they are not easy to escape.

Doctor Tech

Technology plays a key part in looking after us. Smart machines and materials repair or replace damaged body parts. Scanners see inside the body and tell physicians if anything's wrong. Machines allow surgeons to operate on a patient from far away. Robot doctors can even listen to patients to help find the problem.

Camera

Transmitter

Receiver implant inside eye

Passive bionics with a single purpose, such as a heart and hip joint

Active bionics with multiple purposes

Bionic body parts

When something is wrong with part of your body or it is lost, maybe you can replace it with a mechanical "bionic" part? Some people already have artificial hearts, livers, legs, arms, and ears. One day, these parts may work better than the real thing, giving people superpowers. Blind people may one day be given sight by implanted video cameras (above).

A magnetic field pulls hydrogen particles in the body into alignment.

When the field is switched off, the scanner picks up the pattern of tiny radio signals that the particles send out as they swivel back to normal.

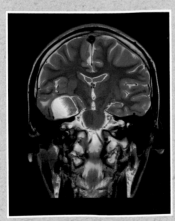

Inside view

Physicians can look inside your body to see if anything's wrong with smart scanners. CT (computerized tomography) scanners circle the patient, firing X-ray beams to make computer-generated images. These can reveal cancers and internal injuries. MRI (Magnetic Resonance Imaging) scanners can see things happening in your living brain.

Surgery at a distance

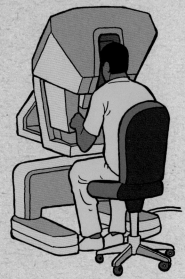

Remote surgery technology could enable surgeons to carry out complex operations on patients from the other side of the world. Robot machinery at the location actually works on the patient. But the surgeon guides it from far away, using **virtual reality** technology.

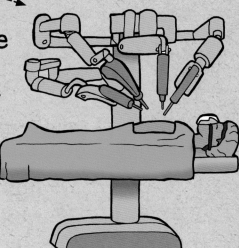

New for old

In the past, replacement body parts were made from materials such as metal or plastic. Now biotechnologists are learning to grow new body parts from living cells, so that they are just like the real thing. These are the stages in growing a whole new nose.

1 A scan builds a three-dimensional (3D) picture of the nose wanted.

2 A 3D honeycomb mold is made using a 3D printer.

3 Special "stem" cells from the body are sprayed onto the mold.

4 The mold is dipped in nutrients so the cells grow into a cartilage nose.

5 The cartilage nose is attached to the body so that skin grows over it.

6 The new, skin-covered nose is secured in place by surgeons.

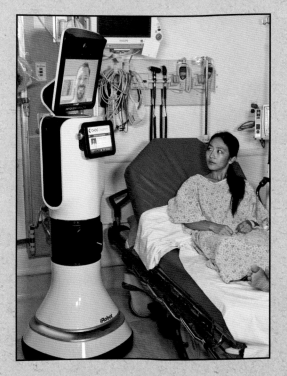

Doctor, doctor

Doctors are busy. So some people think that in future when you go to see a physician, you'll see a robot instead. The robot will ask questions and take measurements, then diagnose the problem and decide the treatment, or send you to a human physician.

Out of This World

Some of the most amazing technology is literally out of this world—it is the technology that has enabled us to explore space. Things that were once just science fiction are now reality, such as living in space stations far above Earth. One day, we may be able to send robots to mine asteroids or take day-trips into space.

International Space Station

Space room

The International Space Station was carried into space piece by piece and put together over dozens of space flights. It now circles the globe every 90 minutes at a speed of about 17,500 miles per hour (28,000 km/h). It is as big as a football field and zooms around Earth at about 250 miles (400 km) above the ground. Since 2009, it usually has had a crew of six staying there four to six months at a time.

Looking into the distance

Earth's atmosphere looks clear to us, but if you want to see faint, distant stars, it's like frosted glass. So astronomers send up special telescopes on satellites to look out from high above the atmosphere in space. The most famous of these space telescopes is the Hubble, launched in 1990. It is still sending back amazing pictures of galaxies right across the other side of the universe.

Hubble space telescope

Hubble image of the Horsehead Nebula

Space vacations

Spaceflights are usually government projects, and outsiders are allowed aboard by special invitation. But space technologists are working on spacecraft that might take ordinary paying customers into space. Virgin Galactic's *SpaceShip Two* will carry six passengers and could be in operation by 2020. But tickets will cost $250,000.

Out and about

Space may be empty, but it is a dangerous place for humans, full of harmful rays and entirely lacking air. So if astronauts need to get outside their spacecraft to make repairs, they wear elaborate protective suits called extravehicular mobility units (EMUs).

A heavy backpack contains air for breathing and water for cooling, as well as jetpacks.

Gold in the visor filters out dangerous rays from the sun.

Multiple layers protect the body from pressure problems, while tubes of circulating water help to stop the body from boiling.

The outer layers protect the astronaut from harmful rays.

Asteroid idea

Asteroids are rich in rare minerals, such as gold, iridium, palladium, platinum, and tungsten. Engineers are working on ways to build robot spacecraft that could be sent to asteroids, extract the minerals, then send them back to Earth on carrier spacecraft. But this is such an expensive process that it probably won't be worthwhile for a while.

Other Worlds

Imagine riding a tiger or seeing a whale leap through your bedroom floor. Well, soon you may be able to have these seemingly lifelike experiences. Computer technology can create these experiences, then immerse us in them so convincingly that they seem real.

Virtual reality

Virtual reality tricks your mind into thinking things are real by feeding signals to your senses. The main way is through stereoscopic display, which gives two slightly different views to each of your eyes. The views shift exactly as if things are real and solid—and change exactly as if you are moving through the scene for real. Some devices also move and shake your body to build up the whole illusion.

Lenses

Display

Circuit board

Solid light

Holograms are 3D photos made with laser beams. The beams are split in two with mirrors and lenses. One bounces off the subject being photographed and onto a photo receiver. The other, called the reference beam, shines directly onto the receiver. The "interference" between the light waves in the two beams creates tiny stripes on the photo receiver. These create a shimmering effect in the photo that looks 3D.

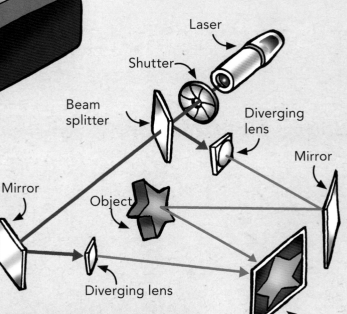

Laser

Shutter

Beam splitter

Diverging lens

Mirror

Mirror

Object

Diverging lens

Receiver for holographic image

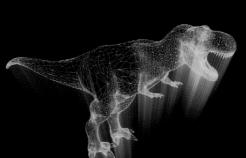

Holographic image

Cyberspace

Cyberspace can simply mean the imaginary place where computer data is shared on the Internet. But it can also mean the creation of new imaginary worlds by interacting computers in a form of virtual reality. Gamers already venture into these worlds when they play together online. You are really just manipulating the gaming controls, put it can seem as if you're fighting your opponent with real swords in a strange world.

Fantasy you

Online, you can already create an imaginary version of yourself called an avatar. You can do this by giving the characteristics you choose to a computer program that behaves like a person. In the future, your avatar might be so realistic and have so much detail about you that it seems real. Who knows, one day you might send your avatar to school while you play at home!

Is that real?

One of the most exciting new technologies is "augmented reality." Unlike virtual reality, it projects amazing computer-generated illusions so that they look as if they are happening in the real world. That's how you might get a whale leaping out of your classroom floor, or keep your own pet dragon under the bed.

About Engineering

Engineers design structures, machines, and materials. They are the people who come up with the directions that tell people how to build and make or shape things, from a giant road tunnel to the pipes in your house.

What do engineers do?

Engineers use science, math, and technical experience to come up with a design for making things. They need to understand the situation properly, then devise a foolproof solution. For example, a heating engineer will design a system that makes sure heat reaches all parts of a building.

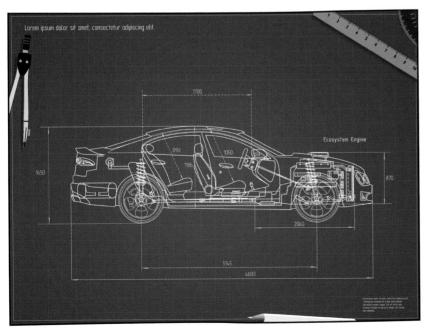

Blueprints

Engineers usually draw their design in a lot of detail, either on paper or on a computer screen. In the past, they drew their plans on paper and copies were made using a process that made the plans blue. These were called blueprints. Even today, when the copies are black-and-white photocopies, engineering plans are often called blueprints.

Computer power

Nowadays, engineers prepare their plans using computer-aided design systems (CAD). These are special programs that let engineers draw their designs in three dimensions on screen and make changes quickly, if needed. Some CAD programs automatically make calculations about stresses and loads. They can also add up the costs of materials as the design is created.

Megaprojects

Some engineering projects are gigantic, taking many years and involving huge numbers of workers and quantities of materials. These megaprojects include the Jubail II industrial city in Saudi Arabia, which involves building a vast city of industrial plants at once. There are 20,000 workers busy trying to get the project finished by 2026.

Three Gorges

Sometimes, giant engineering projects can be controversial. The Three Gorges project in China, which was completed in 2003, created the world's largest dam: 1½ miles (2.4 km) long and about 60 stories high. But its construction involved moving 1.5 million people from their homes and flooding vast areas of farmland.

Holding It Together

Engineers come up with ideas for useful machines, tools, and structures—and then make them. Science, math, and technology are involved, but engineering is really all about making things that work.

Going for growth

Airplane

If you live in a city, you're living in an engineer's world. Everything, from the bridge you cross on the way to school to the rack you hang your coat on when you get there, is the work of an engineer. If you look around you as you travel through a city, you'll see examples of engineering everywhere.

Signal tower

Office building

Ferris wheel

Factory

Bridge

Cars and buses

Power station

Railroad

Chemical cooks

Chemical engineers focus on processes and equipment for making the chemicals we need, from dish-washing detergent to medicines. They work on all scales, but their most obvious work involves creating large factories for making chemicals and oil refineries for processing oil to make fuel and plastics.

Keep it civil

Civil engineers are called "civil" to show they are different from military engineers, who make things for war. Civil engineers make big structures that keep cities going, such as roads, airports, bridges, canals, dams, and buildings. Sometimes, they make huge structures, such as tunnels under the sea or docks large enough for repairing giant oil tankers.

Metallic mechanics

Mechanical engineers are engineers who make machines—anything from cars and buses to door handles and grinders. They make objects that move in some way, and their favorite material is metal, because it is tough and can be shaped however they want.

Sparks

Electrical engineers design and make electrical equipment— that's everything from cell phones to power stations and electric trains. They work with wires, electronic circuit chips, and transistors. They need to be careful so electricity is kept safely out of harm's way by using insulating material or setting wires high up or underground.

Make Up

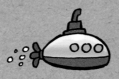

For things to work well, they need to be made from the right material. It would be a waste of time to build a submarine from wood or a hammer from plastic. An engineer has to find the right material for the task, or if the right material doesn't exist, create a new one.

Steel car body

Aluminum radiator

Polycarbonate electrical insulators and reflectors

Polypropylene bumpers (and battery)

Xenon headlights

Leather car seats and fitting

Stainless steel exhaust and trim

Rubber tires (and windshield wipers and hoses)

What's in a car?

Cars need to be superstrong to stand the stresses of engine power. They also need to be a shape that allows space for passengers and components. That's why they're made mostly of steel, which is both strong and easily shaped when hot. But cars include many other materials, such as glass, rubber, and plastic.

Making metals

Metals are used for everything from nails to bridge beams and washing machines to ships. If you heat metal enough, it melts. So you can make it into almost any shape by pouring it into a hollow container called a mold. When it cools, the metal turns hard and solid in the shape of the mold. This is called casting.

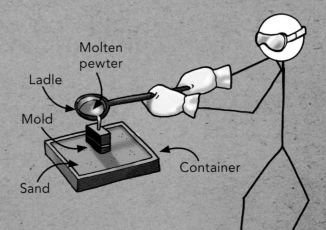

Molten pewter

Ladle

Mold

Sand

Container

Concrete

Typical Concrete Mix

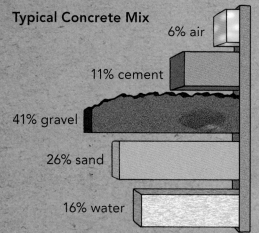

- 6% air
- 11% cement
- 41% gravel
- 26% sand
- 16% water

Concrete was invented long ago, but it is so useful it seems like a new supermaterial. Seven out of ten people in the world live in buildings made at least partly from concrete. It is incredibly strong, especially when reinforced (made stronger) with iron rods. And it is the only building material resistant to fire and water.

Concrete is made by mixing loose sand and gravel, then binding it together with wet powdered cement.

When the cement dries, it sets hard to make solid concrete.

Aggregate (sand and gravel)

Conveyor belt

Concrete supply

Cement store

Concrete mixer truck

Out of oil

Oil is not only a fuel but also a source of an amazing array of materials called petrochemicals. These include everything from the fabric in bedsheets to the plastic in footballs—and even perfumes and medicines. Here are some of the everyday objects made from oil.

Objects made from oil

Materials in a plane, the Boeing 787

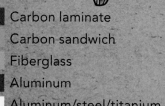

- Carbon laminate
- Carbon sandwich
- Fiberglass
- Aluminum
- Aluminum/steel/titanium pylons

Combined strengths

Composites are amazingly strong, light materials that are made by combining different materials. Typically, they have fibers of glass or carbon embedded in a mass or "matrix" of plastic, metal, ceramic ,or even concrete. The fibers strengthen and stiffen the matrix and help it resist cracks and fractures.
Half of a Boeing 787 airliner is made of composites.

We Got the Power!

When you turn on the lights or the television, you expect electricity to be there to make them work at the flick of a switch. But where does the electricity come from? The answer: It is generated in power stations, then supplied to you through underground wires or overhead cables.

Electricity at home

We use a lot of electricity! The average home around the world uses 3,500 kilowatt hours each year. However, households in the United States use about four or five times the world average! From the moment we get up, we start using electricity for heat, cooking, light, radios, and many other things.

Heat escapes through chimney

Heat escapes through windows

Computer

Loft insulation saves energy

Solar panel creates energy

Light

Hairdryer

Music player

TV and DVD

Shower

Boiler for water and heating

Microwave

Power supply

Wood fire

Refrigerator

Oven

Washing machine

Power network

Power stations use various sources of energy to turn turbines that power **electricity generators**. They send out their electricity through a network of electric cables called a grid.

1 Power station generators are connected to the cables of the grid.

2 To send the electricity long distances, it is boosted to high "voltage" (pressure) by transformers

3 To make the current usable in homes and factories, the voltage is reduced again by more transformers at a substation.

Burn up

Nearly two-thirds of our electricity is made by power stations that burn "fossil fuels." Fossil fuels are coal, oil, and natural gas made from the buried remains of living things. As they burn, they heat water to make steam to turn the generator turbines. But the smoke from burning fossil fuels pollutes the air, which changes the world's climate.

Coal-fired Power Station

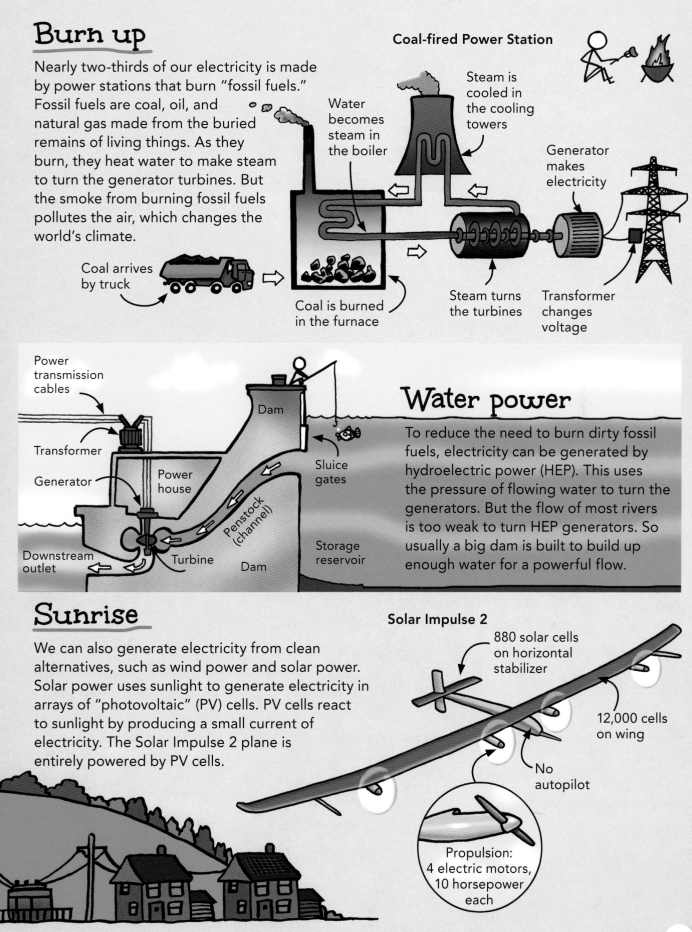

Water becomes steam in the boiler

Steam is cooled in the cooling towers

Generator makes electricity

Coal arrives by truck

Coal is burned in the furnace

Steam turns the turbines

Transformer changes voltage

Water power

To reduce the need to burn dirty fossil fuels, electricity can be generated by hydroelectric power (HEP). This uses the pressure of flowing water to turn the generators. But the flow of most rivers is too weak to turn HEP generators. So usually a big dam is built to build up enough water for a powerful flow.

Power transmission cables

Transformer

Generator

Power house

Dam

Sluice gates

Storage reservoir

Downstream outlet

Turbine

Dam

Penstock (channel)

Sunrise

We can also generate electricity from clean alternatives, such as wind power and solar power. Solar power uses sunlight to generate electricity in arrays of "photovoltaic" (PV) cells. PV cells react to sunlight by producing a small current of electricity. The Solar Impulse 2 plane is entirely powered by PV cells.

Solar Impulse 2

880 solar cells on horizontal stabilizer

12,000 cells on wing

No autopilot

Propulsion: 4 electric motors, 10 horsepower each

55

Building Up

In the last century, engineers have built increasingly taller buildings called skyscrapers. They were originally built to save space in crowded cities. Now many megatall buildings are erected just to show off.

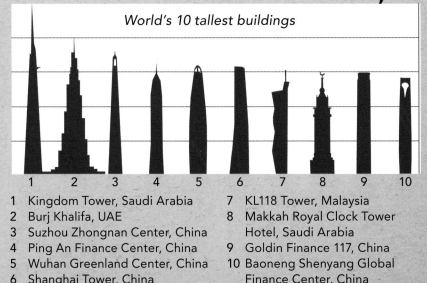

Solar panels collect energy for the building.

Concrete is strengthened with a mat of thin steel fibers.

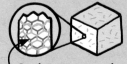

Carbon nanotubes are embedded in the concrete for extra strength.

"Smart" carbon fibers in the concrete send data about stresses.

Electromagnet shafts provide quick escape routes in emergencies.

Elevators can change shafts to stop holdups.

Speedy elevators hauled by carbon-fiber ropes send people up at 60 feet (20 m) per second.

Tall techniques

Most low-level buildings get their strength from brick walls. But megatall buildings have thin walls made mainly of glass, called curtain walls. They get their strength from a superstrong steel frame, or spine, to which concrete floors and the curtain wall are attached. They also incorporate clever new techniques.

Megatall!

The Burj Khalifa in Dubai, at 2,717 feet (828 m) tall and with 163 stories, was the world's tallest building when it opened in 2010. It may lose this title to the Kingdom Tower in Saudi Arabia, which is planned to be more than 3,280 feet (1 km) tall. Here's a comparison with the world's other tallest buildings. Six of them are in China.

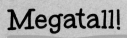

World's 10 tallest buildings

1 Kingdom Tower, Saudi Arabia
2 Burj Khalifa, UAE
3 Suzhou Zhongnan Center, China
4 Ping An Finance Center, China
5 Wuhan Greenland Center, China
6 Shanghai Tower, China
7 KL118 Tower, Malaysia
8 Makkah Royal Clock Tower Hotel, Saudi Arabia
9 Goldin Finance 117, China
10 Baoneng Shenyang Global Finance Center, China

Geometry of the Eiffel Tower

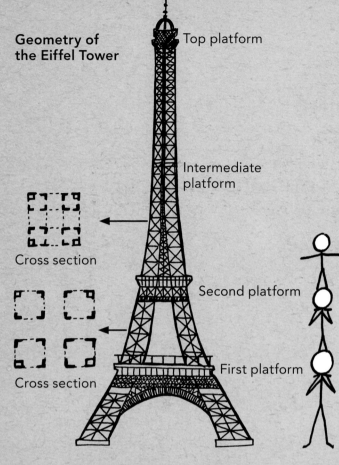

Top platform

Intermediate platform

Cross section

Cross section

Second platform

First platform

Metal shapes

When the Eiffel Tower was built in Paris in 1889, it was the world's tallest man-made structure at 1,063 feet (324 m) tall. Column structures rely on their weight to hold them up. But the Eiffel Tower works by **cantilevers**, which use anchor points. It is made of a geometric lattice of iron girders, each anchored in place by its attachment to others.

Up and around

Not all tall structures are skyscrapers. The Gateway of St. Louis, Missouri, is just an arch for show. But it is the world's tallest, at 630 feet (192 m). It was built out of stainless steel triangular boxes lined with concrete. It has a special mathematical shape, called a catenary, which gives it strength.

The Gateway Arch, St. Louis

Elevator to space

You don't necessarily need a building to have an elevator. Some people think that one day we may build an elevator up into space. A superlight carbon-fiber cable would run from the ground to a weight placed 62,000 miles (100,00 km) above Earth. The weight would hold the cable in place as it orbited our planet. Elevator cars would climb the cable by electromagnets and reach space in a few hours.

Getting Across

Bridges are some of the biggest engineering projects of all—and they are getting bigger all the time. The recently built Danyang-Kunshan Grand Bridge in China carries a high-speed railroad and is more than 102 miles (164.8 km) long.

Bridge types

Bridges used to be built of brick, stone, and iron. Now most are built from concrete and steel. To cross wide rivers or deep gorges, builders usually use **suspension bridges**, which allow for long, high spans.

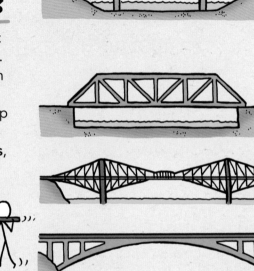

Beam bridges made from rigid beams of steel are simple and effective, but they only work well for short crossings, unless they have support in the middle. **Truss bridges** are made from triangles of steel bars. They are strong and light and are a good design for short crossings.

Cantilever bridges have strong anchor points, with each half of the bridge firmly attached to a support.

Arch bridges made of brick, stone, or concrete are strong but have a limited span, and tall ships may not be able to pass under them.

Suspension bridges have a main span that hangs from cables suspended between tall towers at each end.

Cable-stayed bridges have the main span hanging directly from cables attached to towers.

Towers are constructed on top of steel caissons

Steel caisson

Getting suspended

The key step in building a suspension bridge is setting up the towers at each end. These are tall and take the whole weight of the bridge. So the foundations must be deep and built on solid rock. If the towers have to be in water, engineers start by lowering a vast steel drum called a caisson into the water. The water is pumped out of it and keeps everyone safe and dry while they lay the foundations.

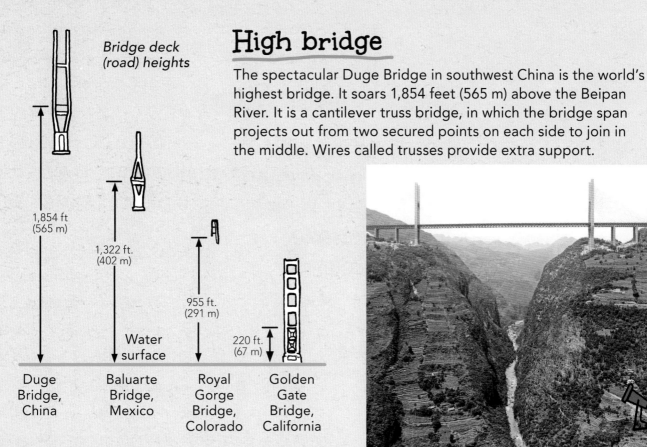

High bridge

The spectacular Duge Bridge in southwest China is the world's highest bridge. It soars 1,854 feet (565 m) above the Beipan River. It is a cantilever truss bridge, in which the bridge span projects out from two secured points on each side to join in the middle. Wires called trusses provide extra support.

Bridge deck (road) heights

1,854 ft (565 m)

1,322 ft. (402 m)

955 ft. (291 m)

Water surface

220 ft. (67 m)

Duge Bridge, China

Baluarte Bridge, Mexico

Royal Gorge Bridge, Colorado

Golden Gate Bridge, California

Duge Bridge

Italian bridge

Perhaps the most famous and beautiful bridge in the world is the Rialto in Venice. It was designed by Antonio de Ponte and built between 1588 and 1591. To support the weight of this stone bridge, the builders had to push more than 12,000 wooden stumps into the mud. Rows of stores selling fine fabrics, jewelry, and glass occupy the colonnade that sits on the bridge.

Scotland's Forth

When it was built in 1881, Scotland's railroad bridge over the Forth estuary near Edinburgh was the engineering marvel of the age. Built entirely of steel girders, it was the world's longest cantilever bridge. Triangles of steel are anchored to two piers and carry the weight by their leverage.

Fly Me

One of the newest of all engineering skills is aeronautical engineering, the engineering of aircraft. The Wright brothers made the first successful aircraft flight in 1903. But just more than a century later, planes are whisking passengers around the world in hours, and there are flying cars that could land in your yard.

Air rider

To build a modern airliner, you need three main parts: a **fuselage**, wings, and engines. The fuselage is the long tube where the pilot, passengers ,and luggage are carried. Two big wings on each side lift the aircraft, and two little wings and a rudder at the rear provide control. The engines power the aircraft through the air.

Main wing

Ailerons help the plane to make bank turns.

Wing flaps give extra lift for steeper takeoff and landing.

Rudder

Tail wings

Economy class seating

Undercarriage wheels for landing and takeoff

Business class seating

Cockpit or flight deck

Kitchen galley

Jet engines on each wing give power.

Supertube

The fuselage of an airliner is essentially a tube of superlight, superstrong materials: mainly aluminum, but also titanium and special composite materials, such as carbon fiber. There is a framework of long beams or "stringers" running along the plane, and a series of hoops or "chords" running around it. Metal panels are secured to the framework to form a "skin."

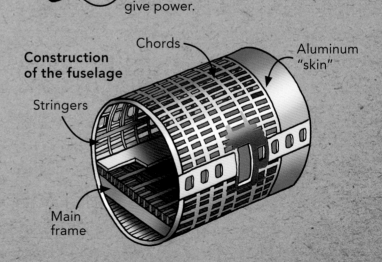

Construction of the fuselage

Chords

Aluminum "skin"

Stringers

Main frame

Wired for flight

When a pilot moves the controls to change direction, a computer sends electrical signals through the wires to motors (actuators) that swivel flaps on the wings. This is called "fly-by-wire." In autopilot, the pilot can leave the controls altogether and the computer makes adjustments to the flight automatically in response to data from the instruments.

How fly-by-wire controls work

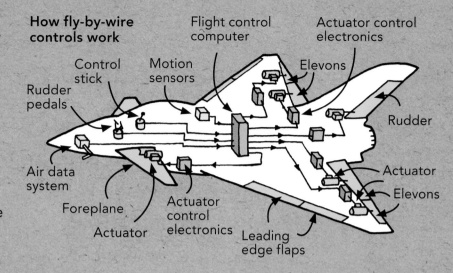

Flight control computer

Actuator control electronics

Control stick

Motion sensors

Elevons

Rudder pedals

Rudder

Air data system

Actuator

Elevons

Foreplane

Actuator

Actuator control electronics

Leading edge flaps

Flight deck

Airline pilots face a dazzling array of instruments in a plane. The display is sometimes called a "glass cockpit," because of all the glass screens showing data readouts, computer updates, and the flight path. The key display is for the FMS (flight management system) computer that automates much of the flight, using satellite and other data to guide the plane on its path.

Jet power

Most modern airliners are powered through the air by jet engines called **turbofans**. All jets have fans that whir around inside a tube, gulping in air. Turbofans have a second giant fan at the front to suck air in. Because some air bypasses the main fans, the engine runs more quietly at takeoff speeds.

1 Some of the air is blown into the engine's main fans, but some bypasses them.

2 Jet fuel is squirted into air squeezed by the main "compressor" fan (indicated) and set alight.

3 The burning fuel expands and rushes past a turbine, setting it spinning.

4 The hot gases shoot out a jet that thrusts the plane forward.

Keeping Afloat

Some ships are the biggest machines of all, and they have to face some of the toughest conditions in the world when they sail into an ocean storm. So a lot of engineering know-how goes into designing and building them. Engineers who work with ships are called marine engineers.

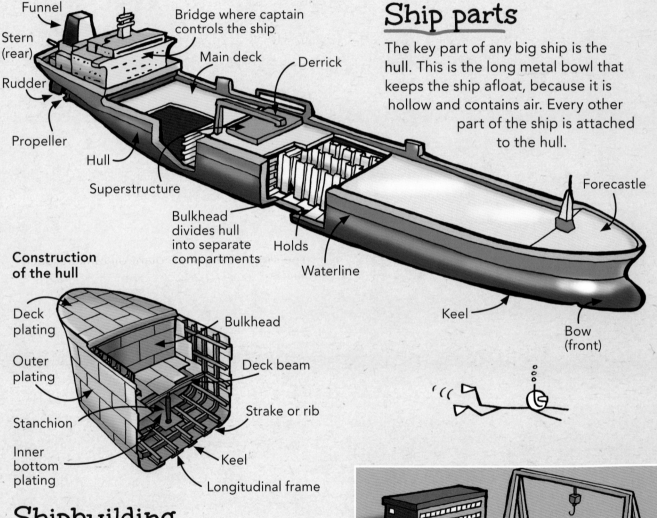

- Funnel
- Stern (rear)
- Rudder
- Propeller
- Hull
- Superstructure
- Bridge where captain controls the ship
- Main deck
- Derrick
- Bulkhead divides hull into separate compartments
- Holds
- Waterline
- Keel
- Forecastle
- Bow (front)

Ship parts

The key part of any big ship is the hull. This is the long metal bowl that keeps the ship afloat, because it is hollow and contains air. Every other part of the ship is attached to the hull.

Construction of the hull

- Deck plating
- Outer plating
- Stanchion
- Inner bottom plating
- Bulkhead
- Deck beam
- Strake or rib
- Keel
- Longitudinal frame

Shipbuilding

Modern cruise ships are put together like cars. The shipbuilders do not make every part of the ship from scratch. Instead, they use a "modular" approach. This means they bring in already made components, such as passenger cabins and giant sections of steel hull. The components are slowly assembled in a shed until the ship is ready to launch into the water for the finishing stages.

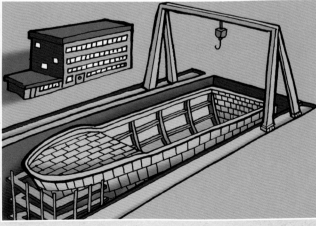

Boxing smart

Bulk cargo is items, such as oil and minerals, that can simply be poured into the ship's hold. But loose cargo—objects of all shapes and sizes—poses a problem. The solution is to put it inside standard metal boxes called containers. This way it can be stacked high in specialized ships that are easy to load and unload. This idea works so well that most nonbulk cargo is now carried in container ships.

Pioneering Spirit

Pioneering Spirit — Empire State Building

World's longest ships

Oil tanker — 1,500 ft. (458 m)

Container ship — 1,309 ft. (399 m)

Bulk carrier — 1,187 ft. (362 m)

Passenger ship — 1,181 ft. (360 m)

Aircraft carrier — 1,118 ft. (341m)

Megaship

The biggest ships are giant oil tankers, such as the *Seawise Giant*, at more than 1,476 feet (450 m) long and weighing well over half a million tons! But the *Pioneering Spirit* is ginormous, too. It is built for lifting and taking away offshore oil rigs that need replacing. *Pioneering Spirit* is 1,253 feet (382 m) long and 406 feet (124 m) wide. See how it compares with the Empire State Building in New York.

Superyacht

In the future, boats may look different. With the latest light, strong materials, such as carbon composites, which can be molded into different shapes, boats can be made in interesting new designs. It's just an idea right now, but the *Trilobis*, for instance, has a transparent underwater section, and a silent, nonpolluting hydrogen engine, so passengers can observe sea life from close up.

Keep Moving

There are well over one billion cars on the world's roads right now, with 263 million in the United States alone. That's one car for almost every American. So automotive engineers, who design and make cars, buses, and trucks, have a lot of work.

Car parts

Modern cars are complicated machines. But most have the same elements: four wheels, a body to carry passengers, an engine to power the wheels, and controls for the driver. The car's power typically comes from burning gasoline or diesel inside the engine. It expands and pushes firmly on a piston, which turns the shafts that drive the wheels around.

Drive shaft takes the engine's power to the rear wheels

Fuel tank holds the fuel for the engine

Driver's seat

Steering wheel

Engine provides power to move the car

Battery holds store of electricity for when engine is not running

Suspension soaks up bumps in the road

Brake discs give a surface for the brakes to grip and stop the car

Wheels carry the car forward

Exhaust pipe takes away hot waste gases from the engine

Keeping safe

Nearly 1.3 million people are killed in car accidents every year. So car engineers include features to protect passengers in case of a crash.

Steering column collapses quickly in a crash to avoid crushing the driver

Crumple zone at the front, designed to crumple easily and soak up some of the impact

Safety glass breaks into beads instead of sharp splinters

Airbags inflate rapidly to provide a cushion for passengers

Passenger cell, a cage of strong bars, protects the passenger compartment

Safety belts stop passengers form hurtling forward violently

Half clean

When gasoline and diesel engines burn fuel, they chuck out a lot of dirty gases that not only damage people's health but the world's climate, too. So, many carmakers are looking for cleaner ways to power cars. One well-tried idea is the hybrid. This has both a gasoline engine and an electric motor, sharing the task of powering the car.

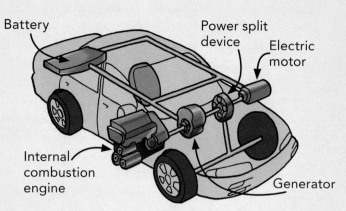

Battery

Power split device

Electric motor

Internal combustion engine

Generator

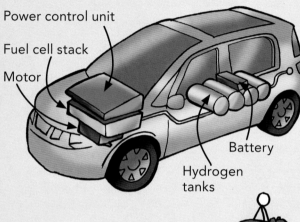

Power control unit

Fuel cell stack

Motor

Battery

Hydrogen tanks

Water works

Another idea for cleaner engines is the **hydrogen fuel cell**. In some ways, these are like batteries powered by hydrogen. Hydrogen is flammable, but here it is not burned. Instead, it is combined with oxygen in a process that makes electricity to power an electric motor. Combining oxygen and hydrogen makes water, so the only waste from hydrogen cells is pure water.

Giant dumper

The biggest dump truck of all is the BelAZ 75710 made in Belarus. It can move almost 550 tons (500 metric tons) of rubble in a single load—about the weight of 250 cars or 40 African elephants. To move all that, it has an engine with a torque (turning force) of 13,738 pounds per foot (18,626Nm)—about 24 times what a 2014 Formula One racing car can do.

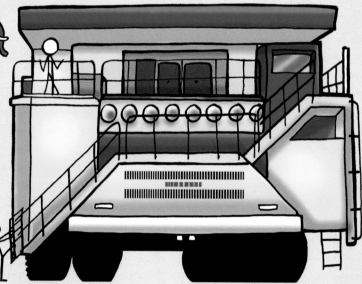

Shock speed

"Shockwave" is the world's fastest truck. From the front, it looks like an ordinary 1984 Peterbilt truck. But three Pratt & Whitney jet engines at the back blast this monster from a standstill to 300 miles per hour 480 km/h) in just 11 seconds. And it can scorch along at 376 miles per hour (605 km/h)!

On Line

Since the first railroad was built just under 200 years ago, engineers have laid 1.4 million miles (2.25 million km) of iron and steel track around the world. Railroads are being built all the time—under cities and through mountains, across rivers and deserts.

Pantograph picks up electric power from overhead cables.

Driver's cab

Streamlined nose

Transformer converts the high-voltage supply from overhead cables to low voltage

Power packs supply electric power to four-wheel swiveling "trucks"

Trucks carry electric "traction" motors that drive the wheels

Motor circuits control the flow of electricity and speed of the motors.

Fast train

High-speed trains are the fastest way of getting around without actually flying. The fastest trains can reach speeds of 350 miles per hour (560 km/h, much faster than a Formula One racing car. They are powered by electric motors and run on special tracks with only gentle curves.

Cutting edge at the front with whirring blades that slice through solid rock

Conveyor belt takes waste rock out of the tunnel

Going under

In 2016, the Gotthard rail tunnel, the world's longest, was completed under the Alps mountain range in Switzerland. It is more than 35 miles (57 km) long. Tunnels like this are bored out with huge machines called tunnel boring machines (TBM), which are like giant drills.

Cutting edge moves slowly forward as rock is bored

Premade concrete ring sections are automatically pushed into place as the head moves forward

Magnetic rise

The fastest trains have no wheels or engine. They are called **maglevs** (short for "magnetic levitation") and use the power of magnetism to float above the track. In 2015, an experimental Japanese maglev reached 375 miles per hour (603 km/h).

Magnets propel the train forward as well as lift it.

Powerful "superconducting" magnets

Train floats inside a guideway of magnets

Magnets in both train and track

ZOOM!

Future train?

The **hyperloop** is an idea for a superfast train. The aim is to shoot passenger-carrying pods at great speeds through a tube emptied of air, using the power of electromagnets. Test trains have reached speeds of 240 miles per hour (387 km/h). They may one day reach speeds of 700 miles per hour (1,134 km/h).

Making tracks

Trains need tracks to run on. In most designs, flat-bottom steel rails are laid across wooden or concrete support planks called sleepers. The sleepers rest on a bed of crushed stone or "ballast," and the ballast rests on a bed of finer gravel called subgrade.

Gauge

Rails

Sleeper

Tie plates

Ballast

Slope 2:1

Sub-ballast

Filter fabric

Subgrade

Blow Up

Military engineers have always been important for armies. They are sometimes called sappers and it is their task to build things for attack or defense in war. It is also their task to destroy the defenses of the enemy, including walls and minefields.

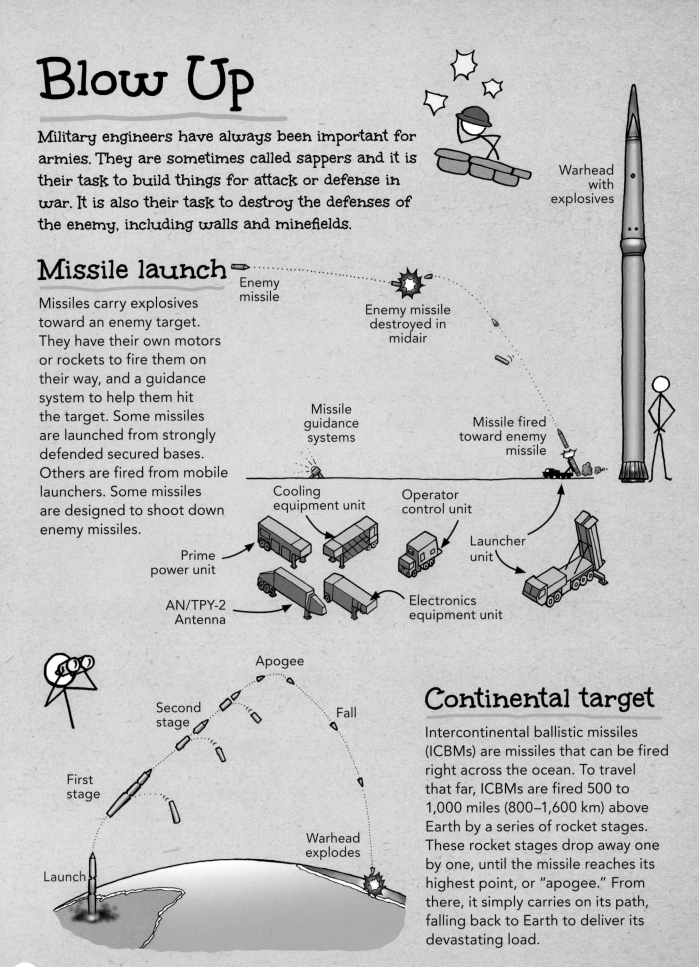

Warhead with explosives

Missile launch

Missiles carry explosives toward an enemy target. They have their own motors or rockets to fire them on their way, and a guidance system to help them hit the target. Some missiles are launched from strongly defended secured bases. Others are fired from mobile launchers. Some missiles are designed to shoot down enemy missiles.

Enemy missile

Enemy missile destroyed in midair

Missile guidance systems

Missile fired toward enemy missile

Cooling equipment unit

Operator control unit

Prime power unit

Launcher unit

AN/TPY-2 Antenna

Electronics equipment unit

Apogee

Second stage

Fall

First stage

Launch

Warhead explodes

Continental target

Intercontinental ballistic missiles (ICBMs) are missiles that can be fired right across the ocean. To travel that far, ICBMs are fired 500 to 1,000 miles (800–1,600 km) above Earth by a series of rocket stages. These rocket stages drop away one by one, until the missile reaches its highest point, or "apogee." From there, it simply carries on its path, falling back to Earth to deliver its devastating load.

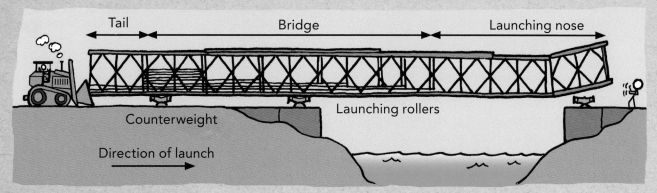

Tail — Bridge — Launching nose

Counterweight

Launching rollers

Direction of launch

Bridge makers

Sometimes armies find themselves with a river to cross—and no bridge. Maybe the enemy has blown up the only one. Then the army calls in the engineers to set up a temporary bridge called a Bailey bridge. This is made of premade sections of "truss" (steel frames) that can be brought to the site on trucks, then secured together quickly.

Commander's machine gun

Hatch

Main gun

Gun sights

Turret that swivels to point the gun

Periscope to help crew see out

Tanks to you

Tanks are mobile fortresses, designed to storm their way across battlefields. They are protected by their huge weight and strong armor. They are also mobile guns that bring huge firepower up close to the enemy. They run on tracks instead of wheels, so they can cross terrain from chilly mud to scorching sand.

Tracks

Engine

Balaklava submarine base

Going to ground

The town of Balaklava on the Black Sea was the site of one of the most amazing feats in military engineering. A network of waterfilled passages allowed submarines to sail far underneath the mountain. This made a submarine base so strong that it could withstand a direct hit from an atomic bomb!

69

About Math

If your eyes glaze over at the mention of math, you're not alone. It can seem a blur of mysterious numbers! But it is one of the smartest of all human skills, and it can do amazing things. And you use it everyday without even realizing it!

What does math do?

Math is like a number sorting machine. You put numbers in, juggle them around, and get different numbers out the other end. The way they come out tells you a lot and can give the solution to a difficult problem. If you want to know how to divide a pizza fairly between friends, math can tell you. If you want to plot your spaceship's course to Mars, math can do that, too!

The math families?

Most of the greatest math brains of the last 300 years came from just 24 sets of teachers and their pupils. In the 1700s and 1800s, most math whizzes, such as Friedrich Liebnitz, were German or Dutch. In the last century, it was the United States that was the math superpower.

Katherine Johnson, an inspiring African-American mathematician, whose work was crucial for the first space flights

Math and computers

Without math, there would be no computers. Computers were invented to make solving mathematical problems easier. A special kind of math is used to develop the programs that control math. And computers are now the best way to solve the most difficult mathematical problems.

Math and science

Many scientists, especially physicists, are mathematicians, too. Math allows you to conduct experiments with objects much too big or dangerous to test for real. If you want to know if a black hole could theoretically suck in a planet, math may give the answer. If you want to see how far the explosion from a nuclear bomb will be felt, you can work it out with math.

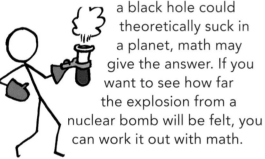

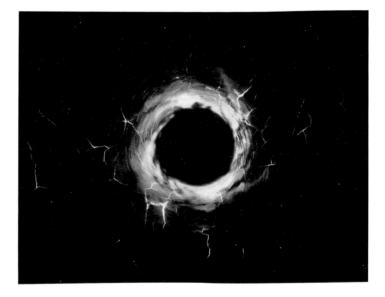

Everyday math

And, of course, you use it all the time in everyday life. Math tells you if you have been given the right change from a store. It tells you how many days of vacation you have. Or how many points your team need to avoid coming bottom of the league!

Making It Count

Without numbers, life would be difficult. You couldn't tell the time. Or know how many brothers and sisters you have. Or how much things cost. Numbers are the basis of mathematics. But where did numbers come from?

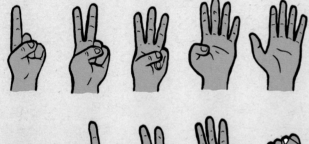

Numbers on hand

When people first started to count, they probably used the most handy thing they could find—their fingers. Even before they had names for numbers, they could simply touch their fingers to count. It is why even today we count in groups of ten, because we have ten fingers.

Making a mark

The problem with finger counting is that there's no way of keeping a record. So about 6,000 years ago, Sumerian farmers began making marks on clay to keep track of things, such as how many bags of corn they'd sold. The smart Egyptians developed a clever system for showing larger numbers with pictures called hieroglyphs.

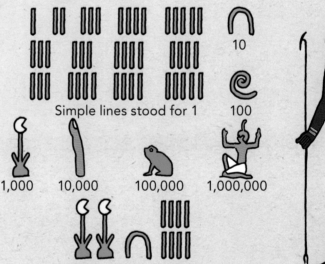

Simple lines stood for 1   10   100

1,000   10,000   100,000   1,000,000

Here's the year **2018** in Egyptian hieroglyphs

X out of ten

The Romans were methodical people. In the time of the Roman Empire, they set up a regular system of numbers shown by letters called numerals. They are still sometimes used today, such as in the names of kings and queens. The British queen is called Elizabeth II, which means the second.

Here's the year **2018** in Roman numerals: MMXVIII

Numbers one to three are capital "i": I, II, III
5 is V
10 is X
4 is IV and 9 is IX
50 is L
100 is C
500 is D
1000 is M

Knowing your place

The system we use today came originally from India. They had a simple system with just 10 symbols, one for each of the numbers from 1 to 10. Bigger numbers are created simply by adding them in the right place. Each extra place multiplies the number by 10.

The year **2018** in modern numerals means
2 x 1000, 0 x 100, 1 x 10, 8 x 1

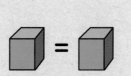

1 one = one

10 ones = 1 ten

Big numbers

Big numbers are used both for things that are really big and things that are small. There is no limit to just how big a number can be. But mathematicians have devised simple shorthands to make really big numbers easier to write down. One is by names for large numbers. The other is by **powers**.

Millions—
population of
New York (8.5)

Billions—
population of
world (7.6)

Trillions—
number of
brain cells (0.1)

Quadrillions—
number of bacillus
that can grow in
one day (16)

Quintillions—
how far away
Andromeda galaxy
is in miles (14)

Sextillions—
grains of sand
on Earth's
beaches

Septillions—
stars in the
universe

Octillions—
mass of
Earth in
grams (5.98)

Nonillions—
atoms in the
human head
(0.45)

Decillions—
mass of the
sun in grams
(15)

Powers of ten

Another way of writing big numbers is to express them in powers of ten.

- One hundred is ten squared (10 x 10) or ten to the power of two. This is written as 10^2.

- One thousand is ten cubed (10 x 10 x 10) or ten to the power of three. This is written as 10^3.

- Ten thousand is 10 x 10 x 10 x 10 or ten to the power of four. This is written as 10^4.

More or Less

Addition and subtraction are the most basic of all mathematical skills and were practiced long ago in prehistoric times. Indeed, it is thought that some animals, including chimpanzees, can perform simple additions and subtractions.

Adding and taking away

Addition means putting two numbers together to get a third, the sum. It is essentially a process of piling up. Subtraction is the opposite of addition. It involves taking one number away from another to give a third number.

With addition, you begin with a pile of 3 socks, add 4 more, and count how many socks you have in total, which is 7 (the sum).

With subtraction, you begin with a pile of 5 socks, take away 2, and count up how many socks you have left, which is 3 (the difference).

Majorities

In democratic countries, many decisions are made by numbers. People vote, and when all the votes are added up, the group or policy with the most votes wins. If you add up all the votes for the winner, then take away all the other votes, the difference is called the "majority."

In the U.S. Congress, there are 435 members of the House of Representatives and 100 members of the Senate.

Members mostly belong to the Republican Party or the Democrats.

- ● Democrats
- ● Republicans

House of Representatives

Senate

If the House of Representatives has 238 Republicans and 193 Democrats (plus 4 Independents), the Republicans have a majority of 238 – 197 = 41

If the Senate has 51 Democrats and 47 Republicans (plus 2 Independents), the Democrats have a majority of 51 – 49 = 2

	~~1~~	~~2~~	~~3~~	~~4~~	~~5~~	~~6~~
~~7~~	~~8~~	~~9~~	10	11	12	13
14	15	16	17	18	19	20
21	22	23	24	25	26	27
28	29	(30)	31			

A difference

For mathematicians, subtraction is the same as addition—except you end up with a "difference," not a sum. The difference is the number you need to add to the subtracted number to give the original number. All computers rely on this way of thinking. Another way of thinking about subtraction is counting backward, such as in the countdown to a rocket launch, or marking the days off a calendar.

Winning the league

Sports leagues are simple examples of addition in action. In soccer, each team gets a certain number of points for each game, depending on the result, such as 3 for a win, 1 for a draw, and 0. Over the season, the points for all their results are added up. The teams are then placed in a league table in points order. The one with most points wins.

LA LIGA

	P	W	D	L	F	A	PTS
BARCELONA	36	26	6	4	10	34	84
REAL MADRID	35	26	6	3	96	39	84
ATLETICO	36	22	8	6	66	25	74
SEVILLA	36	20	9	7	63	45	69
VILLARREAL	36	18	9	9	53	32	63
ATHLETIC CLUB	36	19	5	12	51	39	62

Storekeeper's subtraction

Here's a trick to help with subtracting numbers in your head. It's called the "storekeeper's method" and works by simple counting. If you wanted to take $8.00 from $17.25, for example, work out what number you add to $8.00 to make $17.25 by simply counting on your fingers or in your head, from 8 up to 17.

How Big

By themselves, numbers don't mean much. If your friend asks how much money you have in your pocket, and you say "73," she'd have to say, "73 what?" Did you mean cents, dollars, or squirrel's nuts? So the "what" is important, and mathematicians call this a "unit." With a unit, the number tells you how many, how much, how big.

How big?

A unit can be just an object, like a cow. You might say, there are "5 cows" in the field. But a **unit of measurement** is a standard size that shows how big something is. Units of measurement could be length, weight, volume, and many other things. To record how big you are, you use units of length, such as feet and inches (or centimeters).

How tall are you?

How big is your head?

How big is your waist?

How long are your arms?

How big are your feet?

How long are your legs?

Why not use a tape measure to make these measurements, then compare them with your family or friends?

Little and large

Units of length allow us to say who was the tallest man ever. It was Robert Wadlow (1918–40) of the United States. In meters, he was a lofty 2.72 meters tall. One meter is about 3 feet 3 inches. So he was also 8 feet 11 inches tall. Chandra Dangi (1939–2015) of Nepal was the shortest man ever, at 1 foot 9½ inches (54.6 cm).

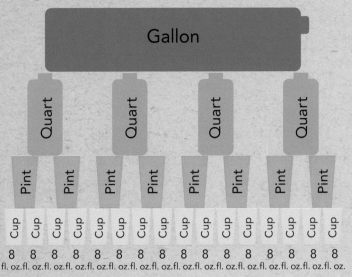

U.S. standard measures for liquids

Gallon

Quart | Quart | Quart | Quart

Pint | Pint | Pint | Pint | Pint | Pint | Pint | Pint

Cup Cup Cup Cup Cup Cup Cup Cup Cup Cup Cup Cup Cup Cup Cup Cup

8 8 8 8 8 8 8 8 8 8 8 8 8 8 8 8
fl. oz.fl. oz.fl. oz.fl. oz.fl. oz.fl. oz.fl. oz.fl. oz.fl. oz.fl. oz.fl. oz.fl. oz.fl. oz.fl. oz.fl. oz.fl. oz.

Setting standards

You can measure things in two main ways: U.S. standard units and metric. In the metric system, units go up in steps of 10 times, 100 times, or 1,000 times; for example, 10, 10, or 1,000 milliliters of a liquid. U.S. standard units are more complex. Here are the measures for liquids: 8 fluid ounces in 1 cup; 2 cups in 1 pint; 2 pints in 1 quart, and 4 quarts in 1 gallon.

Missing Mars

It's really important to know what units of measurement you're using. Three feet is very different from 3 meters. In 1999, NASA's Mars Climate Orbiter space probe burned up in the Martian atmosphere because engineers got their calculations wrong. They had failed to convert from the U.S. customary units to metric.

Mars Climate Orbiter

Laser for measuring a standard meter

Meter

If objects are to be measured accurately in meters, you need to know just how long a meter is. In the past, a meter was the length of a special platinum alloy bar stored safely in Sèvres, France. Now it is set by a laser beam, and is the distance traveled by light in $\frac{1}{299792458}$ second.

Divide and Rule

Multiplying and dividing are two of the key tasks of math. They can sound complicated at first, but they are basically counting in groups. Multiplying is about counting up groups, division is about counting them down.

Multiplying

How many socks will you use in a week if you wear a fresh pair every day? Your group is two socks, a pair. So count or add two socks seven times, once for each day of the week. Mathematicians like to say that's 2 times 7, but it's the same as two 7 times. Every multiplication is the same. You simply add a group a particular number of times. The symbol "x" means times.

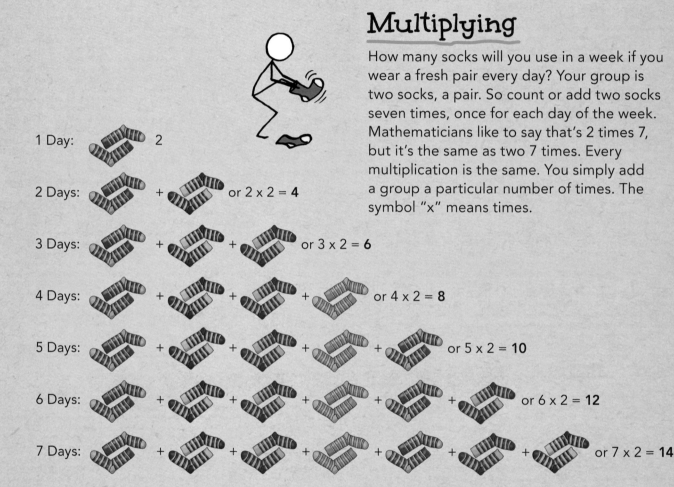

1 Day: 2

2 Days: + or 2 x 2 = **4**

3 Days: + + or 3 x 2 = **6**

4 Days: + + + or 4 x 2 = **8**

5 Days: + + + + or 5 x 2 = **10**

6 Days: + + + + + or 6 x 2 = **12**

7 Days: + + + + + + or 7 x 2 = **14**

Dividing

Dividing is about sharing or counting down. How many days will 14 socks last? Count down or take away two socks (a pair) for each day until you run out of socks.

14 ÷ 2 = **7** or

14 − − − − − − − = **0**

Day 1: 12   Day 2: 10   Day 3: 8   Day 4: 6   Day 5: 4   Day 6: 2   Day **7**: 0

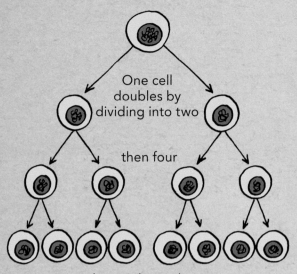

One cell doubles by dividing into two

then four

then eight, and so on

How things grow

Multiplication and division are at the heart of all life. Every living thing, including us, is made of tiny cells. Things grow because these cells are continually splitting into two, or dividing. They grow because by dividing they multiply. One cell divides to become two. Two cells divide to become four. Four cells divide to become eight and so on. Bacteria do this so quickly that one can become many millions in a few hours. This is why illnesses can spread quickly.

People power

If every mother and father had just two children, the population of the world would stay the same. But many moms and dads have more than two. So the world's population is multiplying rapidly. There are now 7.6 billion people in the world. The population grows by 75 million each year.

Projected World Population

Year	Population
1990	5.3 billion
2015	7.3 billion
2030	8.5 billion
2050	9.7 billion
2100	11.2 billion

On average, children around the world can expect to live 622,000 hours (71 years). Some say the oldest person in the world was Li Ching Yuen, who lived 2.24 million hours (256 years). But scientists say that isn't possible.

Dividing time

Time depends on division. Years are divided into 365 days. Days are divided into 24 hours. Hours are divided into 60 minutes. Minutes are divided into 60 seconds. You can see the divisions of the day into hours and minutes clearly on an old-fashioned clock.

Getting the Facts

On their own, numbers mean little. But numbers of something is data, which is a useful way of ordering the world. Data is a collection of facts, such as numbers, words, measurements, observations, or just descriptions of things. You can use math to help you collect data, and then handle the data you collected.

Elephant facts

If you want to know more about an elephant, you can collect two kinds of data. **Qualitative data** describes something in words. **Quantitative data** is in numbers. You can collect quantitative data by either counting or measuring. Here is some data about elephants. See if you can work out what kind of data each is.

African elephant	Asian elephant
Ears: Larger	Ears: Small, rounded
Trunk tip: Two "fingers"	Trunk tip: One "finger"
Head: Single dome	Head: Twin dome
Height: 9–13 feet	Height: 6.5–9 feet
Weight: 8,800–15,400 lb	Weight: 6,500–13,200 lb

Bars and pies

You can simply present your data as lists of numbers, but it is much easier to get the picture if you present it in a graph. **Bar charts** and **pie charts** show the numbers in different groups—bars by the height or length of bars, pie charts by the size of wedge-shaped slices of a pie. Here's a pie chart showing the production and use of oil.

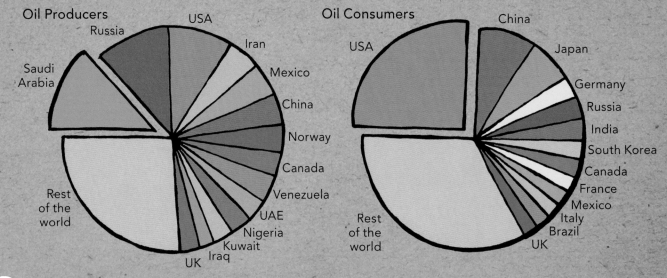

Oil Producers
Russia · USA · Iran · Mexico · China · Norway · Canada · Venezuela · UAE · Nigeria · Kuwait · Iraq · UK · Rest of the world · Saudi Arabia

Oil Consumers
China · Japan · Germany · Russia · India · South Korea · Canada · France · Mexico · Italy · Brazil · UK · USA · Rest of the world

Yellow	||||	4
Blue	⌶⌶⌶	5
Red	⌶⌶⌶ |	6
Pink	|	1
Green	||||	4

Making a survey

Surveys are a great way to learn about the world. Some surveys ask people's opinions through questionnaires and so on. Some find out about things, such as how dirty the air is, by taking measurements. Here's how you might find out about the favorite colors of your classmates. There are four steps to every survey (below left).

1 Think up the question or questions. Here it is "What is your favorite color?"
2 Ask your question. Go around the class asking your question, and record the answers with a mark in the right box.
3 Tally (add up) the results. Add up the totals for each color.
4 Present the results. Make a bar chart in which the height of each bar shows how many like each color.

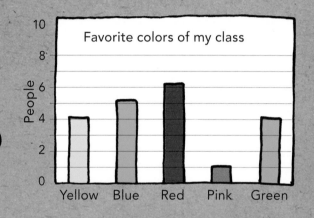

Line up

Line graphs show the varying relationship between two sets of numbers as a sloping line. It is thought that polar bears are suffering because climate change is damaging their Arctic home. So a zoologist might make a line graph to show the changes in average temperature around the world year by year.

1 Using a ruler, make marks for each year along the bottom, and marks for temperature up the side.
2 Make a dot for the temperature in each year.
3 Draw a line joining up the dots.

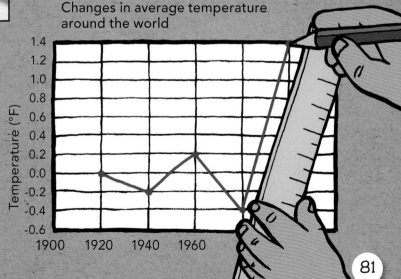

Changes in average temperature around the world

Small Parts

Every number you can count is called a "whole" number. But there are also part numbers called fractions. Fractions are what you get when you divide something in an equal number of parts, whether it is pieces of pizza or different weights.

Piece o' pizza

You can think of fractions as slices of pizza. In every fraction, there are two numbers that matter. The **denominator** is how many equal slices you've cut your pizza into. The **numerator** is how many of those slices you've actually got.

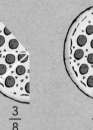

$\frac{1}{4}$
(one-quarter)

$\frac{3}{8}$
(three-eighths)

$\frac{1}{2}$
(one-half)

When you add up fractions, they can sometimes be made into simpler fractions.

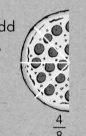

$\frac{4}{8}$
(four-eighths)

$\frac{2}{4}$
(two-quarters)

$\frac{1}{2}$
(one-half)

When you have more than one piece, you get a "mixed fraction."

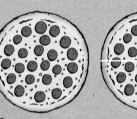

$1\frac{3}{4}$ (one and three-quarters)

Another way to express this is as a fraction called an "improper fraction."

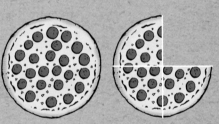

$\frac{7}{4}$ (seven-quarters)

Numbers compared

In this delicious drink recipe, $\frac{4}{5}$ should always be pineapple juice and $\frac{1}{5}$ orange. But it is much easier to think of these fractions as "parts." You then say the recipe is 4 parts pineapple juice to 1 part orange juice. Here, a part is a glass. It doesn't matter what size the glass is, only that there is always four times as much pineapple as orange.

1 Pour 1 glass of orange juice into a pitcher.

2 Add 4 glasses of pineapple juice.

3 Add 1 sprig of fresh cilantro.

4 Stir in 4 teaspoons of honey.

5 Serve with plenty of ice.

By the hundred

To compare things, people often use **percentages**. This just means converting every fraction to hundredths—$\frac{3}{4}$ is the same as $\frac{75}{100}$ or 75 percent (%). To change a fraction to a percentage, use a calculator to divide the top number by the bottom, then multiply by 100. This chart shows the percentage of people at different ages using glasses.

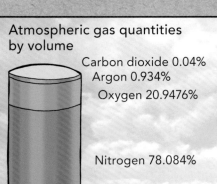

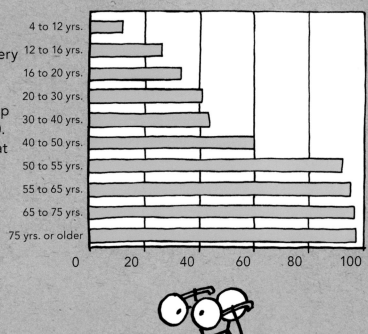

	0	20	40	60	80	100
4 to 12 yrs.						
12 to 16 yrs.						
16 to 20 yrs.						
20 to 30 yrs.						
30 to 40 yrs.						
40 to 50 yrs.						
50 to 55 yrs.						
55 to 65 yrs.						
65 to 75 yrs.						
75 yrs. or older						

Air mix

In any mixture, the proportions of the ingredients are much the same, no matter how much of the mixture you have. The air around us is a mix of gases: oxygen and nitrogen with small amounts of other gases. In this diagram, the proportion of each gas is shown as blocks out of a hundred. These can be written as percentages (see above).

Atmospheric gas quantities by volume

Carbon dioxide 0.04%
Argon 0.934%
Oxygen 20.9476%

Nitrogen 78.084%

Are you concentrating?

Most liquids are either acidic or alkaline. When they are concentrated with a lot more of one than the other—strongly acid or strongly alkaline—they can be dangerous, causing severe burns. Their concentration is measured on the pH scale from 1 to 14. A neutral liquid, such as tap water, has a pH of about 7. The strongest acid has a pH of 0; the strongest alkali has a pH of 14.

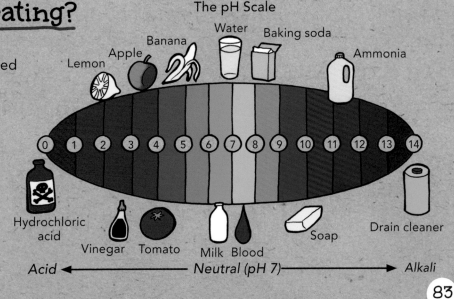

The pH Scale

Lemon   Apple   Banana   Water   Baking soda   Ammonia

0 1 2 3 4 5 6 7 8 9 10 11 12 13 14

Hydrochloric acid

Vinegar   Tomato   Milk   Blood   Soap   Drain cleaner

Acid ←——————— *Neutral (pH 7)* ———————→ *Alkali*

Getting the Point

Fractions can be seriously complicated to work out. That's why decimals are so helpful. The word "decimal" means in tens. In fact, our entire number system is decimal, because it is based on units of ten. But normally when mathematicians talk of decimals, they mean decimal fractions.

Decimating

What decimal fractions do is express every fraction in terms of tenths, hundredths, thousandths, millionths, and so on. And by using a dot called the decimal point after the whole number, fractions can be written as simple digits. One-half is five tenths, or 0.5. One-quarter is 25 hundredths, or 0.25. Three-quarters is 75 hundredths or 0.75.

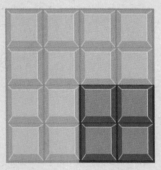
$\frac{1}{4}$ = 0.25

$\frac{1}{2}$ = 0.5

$\frac{3}{4}$ = 0.75

There are 100 pence in 1 pound.

There are 100 cents in 1 dollar and 10 cents in a dime.

There are 100 cents in 1 euro.

Working with decimals

The great advantage of decimal fractions is that they can be worked on in exactly the same way as whole numbers. They work especially well for calculators. That's why most money systems today are decimal. There are 100 cents in the US's 1 dollar, for instance, just as there are 100 cents in Europe's 1 euro, or 100 pence in the UK's 1 pound.

Complicated decimals

To change a fraction to a decimal, divide the figure below the line into the figure above. Some fractions are tricky. To work out the **circumference** of a circle, you multiply its radius by a number called "pi," which has the symbol π, and double it. This is written as C = 2πr. Pi is simple as a fraction: $3\frac{1}{7}$. But in decimals it's a number that goes on forever! However, you can just use 3.142. Phew!

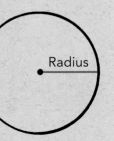
Radius

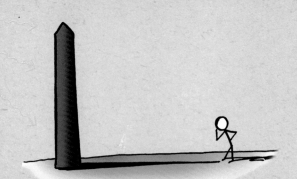

Working out the world

When you're dealing with round things, pi is a big help. Even 2,200 years ago, Greek mathematician Eratosthenes worked out how big Earth is with an ingenious calculation using the shadow cast by a tall tower, the way the sun shone down a deep well, and pi.

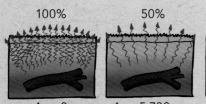
Wood

Leather

Basket

Bones

Just how old

Archaeologists often measure how old things are by carbon dating. Living things all contain a radioactive chemical called carbon 14. This sends out special energy rays. When things die, the carbon 14 in them breaks down at a steady rate. So you can tell the age of objects, such as the remains of wood and plant fibers, from how much carbon 14 they still contain. Decimals make the sums much easier.

100%	50%	25%	12.5%
Age 0	Age 5,730 yrs.	Age 11,460 yrs.	Age 17,190 yrs.

Measuring the breakdown of carbon 14 in a piece of buried wood provides a measurement of the time elapsed since it was living.

Power numbers

The difference in size between an atom and a galaxy is so big we have to write the numbers in shorthand, using powers of ten combined with decimals. Powers are the number of times you multiply a number by itself. One hundred is ten times ten, or ten to the power of two, or 10^2. One thousand is ten times ten times ten, or ten to the power of three, or 10^3. So 1,550,000 is 1.55×10^6.

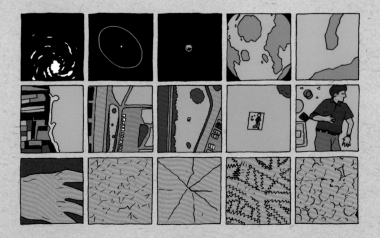

Fast Work

If you want to see how some things compare, you may need ratios and rates. Ratios will tell you whether there are more girls in your class than normal. Rates will tell you whether you can cycle faster than your friends.

Ratio

A ratio is a relationship between two numbers. If you have 2 red apples and 1 green apple in every bag, the ratio is 2 to 1 or 2:1. You probably know that when you were little, the older you got, the fewer teachers you had to look after you. But you can show this mathematically as a changing ratio.

Infants (2–18 months): four babies for each teacher, ratio 4:1

Toddlers (18–36 months): five toddlers for each teacher, ratio 5:1

Preschool (3–5 years): nine children for each teacher, ratio 9:1

Kindergarten and summer school: 12 children for each teacher, ratio 12:1

Heartbeat

A rate is a special kind of ratio. It shows how fast, how many times, or how much something is happening for a particular unit, such as a unit of time or weight. When a physician check your pulse, or heart rate, that person is checking how many times your heart beats every minute — usually 60–100 times a minute when you're relaxed.

Getting littler

When you make an accurate drawing, model, or map, you use another special ratio, called "scale." Scale is the ratio of the length or another measure in the drawing to the length in real life. If a model car is a tenth of the length of the real thing, the scale is 1:10.

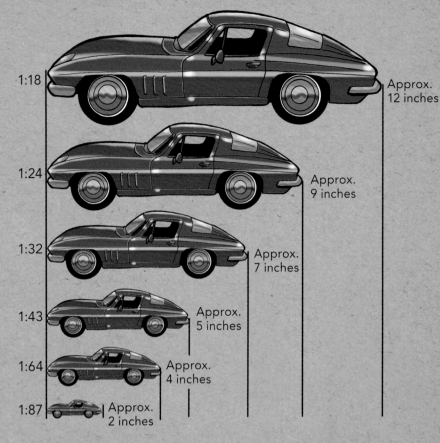

1:18 — Approx. 12 inches

1:24 — Approx. 9 inches

1:32 — Approx. 7 inches

1:43 — Approx. 5 inches

1:64 — Approx. 4 inches

1:87 — Approx. 2 inches

How fast?

Speed is a special kind of rate. It shows the distance traveled in a particular unit of time, typically miles or kilometers per hour (mph or km/h), or feet or meters per second. An athlete might run 400 meters in a minute. That's the same as 24 kilometers per hour, but he couldn't keep that pace up for an hour. In his record 100-meter sprint in 2009, Usain Bolt reached 44.72 km/h (27.8 mph), but for only 20 meters.

Faster and faster

Acceleration shows how quickly something gains speed in a particular unit of time. That means it has the word "per" in it twice. A car might accelerate from a standstill to 60 miles per hour in 10 seconds. So it gains 6 mph in speed in every second, or 6 miles per hour per second. Racing sports cars can accelerate from 0–60 mph in under 3 seconds . . . 1, 2, 3!

A speedometer shows how fast a vehicle is traveling.

Shaping Up

Angles are the cornerstone of the branch of math called geometry. Whenever two straight lines meet, there is an angle between them. Regular angles are found throughout the natural world, in honeycombs, crystals, and atoms. They are used in the construction of everything from household furniture to huge suspension bridges.

Regular shapes

There are many geometric shapes. They are all made by different combinations of straight lines and curves. They can be either flat shapes that you can draw on paper, such as squares and circles, or solid shapes such as spheres (balls), cones, or cylinders. Designers need to know how much material they'll need to make certain shapes. Here are some shapes, and some of the formulas used to work out the areas.

Key: A = area
s = side
w = width
l = length
b = base
h = height
r = radius
d = diameter

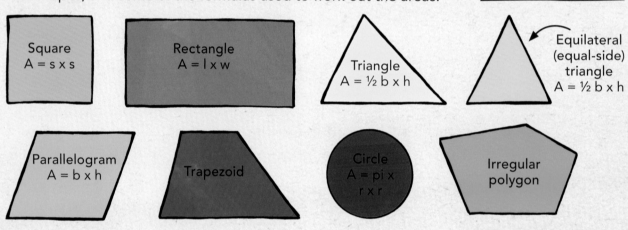

Square
A = s x s

Rectangle
A = l x w

Triangle
A = ½ b x h

Equilateral (equal-side) triangle
A = ½ b x h

Parallelogram
A = b x h

Trapezoid

Circle
A = pi x r x r

Irregular polygon

How much paint?

Area is the amount of space taken up by a particular flat shape. It is simplest to calculate area for a square, so usually it is measured in units, such as square feet or square meters. Area calculations are involved in everything from working out how much material is needed to make a dress to calculating the value of an area of farmland.

To calculate how much paint you need to paint your bedroom:

1 Measure how long the longest and shortest walls are, and add the two lengths: l + w =

2 Measure or guess the height of the wall: h =

3 Multiply the sum of the wall by 2. So 2 x (l + w) =

4 Multiply your answer by the wall height, to give the area of all four walls. 2 x (l + w) x h = area

The paint store will tell you how much paint you need to cover the area you worked out.

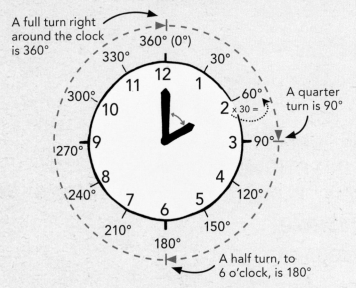

A full turn right around the clock is 360°

360° (0°)
330°
300°
270°
240°
210°
180°
150°
120°
90°
60°
× 30 =
30°

A quarter turn is 90°

A half turn, to 6 o'clock, is 180°

Around the clock

Think of angles like the two hands of an old-fashioned clock, with the hour hand stuck on 12. As the minute hand moves, the angle between the two hands gets bigger and bigger. But angles are measured not in hours and minutes but degrees, usually written with the symbol °.

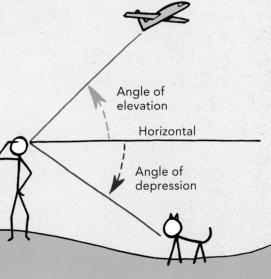

Angle of elevation

Horizontal

Angle of depression

Positive or negative?

An angle can be thought of as the rotation of one line relative to another. If the angle is measured counterclockwise, it is called a positive angle, and if measured clockwise, it is called a negative angle. Similarly, if an angle is measured upward it is called the angle of elevation; if it is measured downward it is called the angle of depression.

What's your angle?

Different names are used to describe different angles and different parts of an angle.

A right angle is when there is a quarter turn, creating a square corner (90°)

An acute angle is a turn less than 90°

An obtuse angle is a turn between 90° and 180°

A reflex angle is a turn between 180° and 360°.

Looking acute

Image

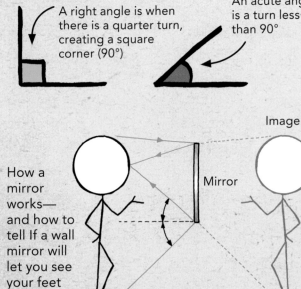

How a mirror works—and how to tell If a wall mirror will let you see your feet

Mirror

You see yourself reflected in a mirror because the light rays hit the mirror and bounce back. They bounce back at the same angle that they hit the mirror, but opposite. You can use this to work out if a wall mirror is long enough to show you all the way down to your feet. The bottom of the mirror—the lowest you can see—must be more than halfway to the floor from your eyes.

Letters Count

In a kind of math called algebra, you work things out by using letters that stand in for unknown numbers. The mystery letters, typically x, y, or z, are known as variables, because they can be any number. When mathematicians need to find out what the mystery number is, they put the letter in a special kind of sum called an equation.

Keeping things equal

An equation is a way of saying that two things are equal. So it always has two halves, with an equals sign in between. A simple equation might be 2 + 3 = 5. In algebra, 3 might be the unknown number, so the equation would be 2 + x = 5. Your job is to solve the equation to find the mystery number x. Here are some famous equations.

Einstein's famous equation $e = m \times c^2$ revealed the relationship between energy (e) and mass (m).

One of Newton's famous equations showed how much gravity makes things accelerate.

Another of Newton's equations was F (Force) = m x a (acceleration), which shows how much force anything moving has.

Pythagoras's theorem $a^2 + b^2 = c^2$ showed how, if you know the length of two sides of a right-angle triangle, you can work out the length of the third side.

Pool power

An algebraic equation is like a pair of weighing scales that must always be balanced. If you do something to one side of the equation, you must do exactly the same to the other side to keep it balanced. In this simple problem, you set up 12 balls on a pool table and put one into a pocket after another until you have just 7 left. How many balls did you pocket?

- If x is the number you pocketed, the equation is $7 + x = 12$
- To find what x is equal to, you can take 7 from each side of the equation, keeping it balanced: $x = 12 - 7$
- The answer is of course 5.

Gravity

Vh

Skate power

Algebra and equations can be used to work out anything from the area of a football field to what electric current you need to make a light glow. They can also be used to understand how different quantities relate to each other, such as how a skateboarder does tricks, such as the hippie jump. This involves him jumping up and landing back on the board, because his speed or "velocity" forward (Vh) matches that of the board.

Beginning the universe

Algebra and equations have enabled scientists to work out just how the universe began, although they can never go back and see for themselves. The math is very complicated, but by adjusting the equations for things we know today, they can wind the clock back to see the forces in play at the dawn of time.

Expanding and cooling universe

The Big Bang theory

9 billion years later, the solar system and Earth begin to form

300 million years later, stars and galaxies begin to form

380,000 years later, electrons and nuclei combine with atoms

First seconds after Big Bang: birth of subatomic particles

13.8 billion years ago: Big Bang

Index

The Author

John Farndon is Royal Literary Fellow at City&Guilds in London, UK, and the author of a huge number of books for adults and children on science, technology, and history, including such international best-sellers as *Do Not Open* and *Do You Think You're Clever?* He has been shortlisted six times for the Royal Society's Young People's Book Prize, for titles such as *How the Earth Works* and *What Happens When?*

The Illustrator

Self-taught comic artist Joe Matthews drew Ivy The Terrible, Ball Boy, and Billy Whizz stories for the *Beano* before moving on to *Tom and Jerry* and *Baby Looney Tunes* comics. He also worked as a storyboard artist on the BBC TV series, *Bob the Builder*. Joe has produced his own *Funny Monsters Comic* and in 2016, published his comic-strip version of the Charles Dickens favorite, *A Christmas Carol*. Joe lives in North Wales, UK, with his wife.

Picture Credits

t = top, m = middle, b = bottom, l = left, r = right.

Shutterstock: 11tl; 11tr; Anatomy Insider 25br; Anna_Pushkareva 7tr; AntonSokolov 12br; Bo1982 6ml; chromatos 29br; Digital Storm 9tl; Dragon Images 23tl; dmitry mokshin 29tl; Eugene Ivanov 28mr; Everett Historical 6bl, 28bl, 29m; Georgios Kollidas 29tr; goodluz 6mr; Gorodenkoff 7ml; halitomer 28tl; LightField Studios 11br; Michelangelus 28tr; Morphart Creation 29mr; niall dunne 19ml; Olga Popova 28ml; Ondrej Prosicky 21mr; Panos Karas 7br; Pictureguy 17br; Sarun T 15br; spatuletail 29bl; YANGCHAO 28br. 927 Creation 47tr; Anton Gvozdikov 36mr; Chaplin 29tl; Chesky 27tr; chombosan 27ml; Dmitry Chulov 33br; Donatas Dabravolskas 46ml; Everett l; Heiti Paves 33ml; Igor Barin 37ml; jennyt 29tr; ksenia_bravo 47ml; Lisa S. 41br; Lukasz Pawel Szczepanski 44br; MriMan 42bl; ; Ociacia 27br; Romolo Tavani 39bl; Scharfsinn 26br; A.Sontaya 49bl; ; Vandrage Artist 46b; Atosan 19ml; cocozero 51br; Denys Po 48bl; Gimas 49ml; Gorodenkoff 49tr; jejim 49br; Kostenko Maxim 48tr; Paul Drabot 45bl; Ross Strachan 49bl;; STLJB 47mr; VPales 69bl; **highestbridges.com:** 69tr, **NASA/restored by Adam Cuerden:** 70bl. **Shutterstock:** 4 PM production 71tl; Alones 70tr; Billion Photos 74bl; Christian Bertrand 75mr; FloridaStock 81bl; Jatuporn Chainiramitkul 75bl; poomooq 83m; Rawpixel 83tl; Vadim Sadovski 7mr. **Wikimedia Commons:** 9br, 53tl

Every effort has been made to trace the copyright holders. And we acknowledge in advance for any unintentional omissions. We would be pleased to insert the appropriate acknowledgment in any subsequent edition of this publication

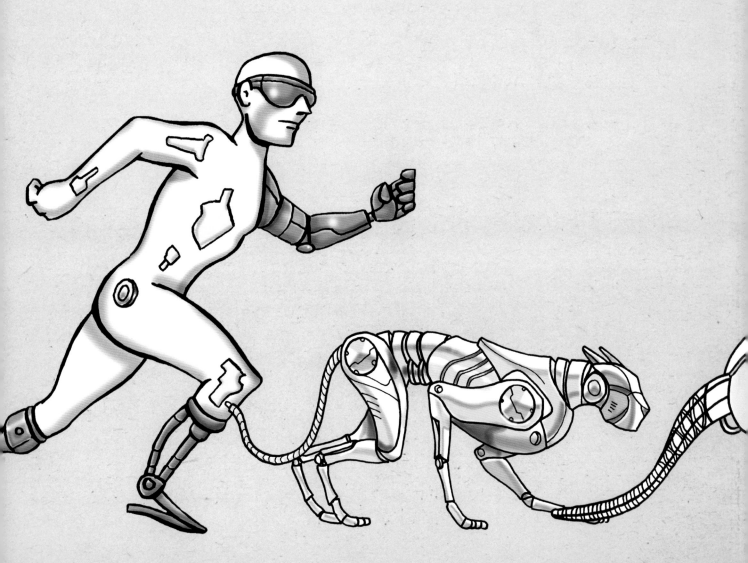